RICHARD WEEK-BY-WEEK

RICHARD WEEK-BY-WEEK

MELANIE KLEIN'S *NARRATIVE OF A CHILD ANALYSIS*

Donald Meltzer

THE HARRIS MELTZER TRUST

Richard Week-by-Week first published in 1978 by Clunie Press for
The Roland Harris Educational Trust
Combined edition of *Freud's Clinical Development, Richard Week-by-Week,*
and *The Clinical Significance of the Work of Bion* published in 1998 by Karnac Books
as *The Kleinian Development.* Reprinted in 2008 for The Harris Meltzer Trust.
New edition 2018 by The Harris Meltzer Trust
60 New Caledonian Wharf
London SE16 7TW

British Library Cataloguing in Publication Data
A C.I.P. for this book is available from the British Library

ISBN 978 1 912567 54 6

Edited, designed and produced by The Bourne Studios
www.bournestudios.co.uk
Printed in Great Britain

www.harris-meltzer-trust.org.uk

CONTENTS

Donald Meltzer (1923–2004) was born in New York and studied medicine at Yale. After practising as a psychiatrist specialising
in children and families, he moved to England to have analysis
with Melanie Klein in the 1950s, and for some years was a train-
ing analyst with the British Society. He worked with both adults
and children, and was innovative in the treatment of autistic children; in the treatment of children he worked closely with Esther
Bick and Martha Harris whom he later married. He taught child
psychiatry and psychoanalytic history at the Tavistock Clinic. He
also took a special scholarly interest in art and aesthetics, based
on a lifelong love of art. Meltzer taught widely and regularly in
many countries, in Europe, Scandinavia, and North and South
America, and his books have been published in many languages
and continue to be increasingly influential in the teaching of
psychoanalysis.

His first book, *The Psychoanalytical Process,* was published by
Heinemann in 1967 and was received with some suspicion (like
all his books) by the psychoanalytic establishment. Subsequent
books were published by Clunie Press for the Roland Harris
Educational Trust which he set up together with Martha Harris

(now the Harris Meltzer Trust). The *Process* was followed by *Sexual States of Mind* in 1973, *Explorations in Autism* in 1975 (with contributions from John Bremner, Shirley Hoxter, Doreen Weddell and Isca Wittenberg); *The Kleinian Development* in 1978 (his lectures on Freud, Klein and Bion given to students at the Tavistock); *Dream Life* in 1984; *The Apprehension of Beauty* in 1988 (with Meg Harris Williams); and *The Claustrum* in 1992. *The Educational Role of the Family: A Psychoanalytical Model* (commissioned for the OECD with Martha Harris) and first published in French in 1976; a new English edition was published in 2013. As a result of his worldwide teaching several compilations exist of his supervision seminars, including *Meltzer in Barcelona* (2002), *Meltzer in Venice* (2016), *Meltzer in Sao Paulo* (2017), *and Meltzer in Paris* (2017). Other accounts by some who use his work in their own teaching practice are in *Teaching Meltzer* (2015). An introductory selection from his writings may be found in *A Meltzer Reader* (2012) and sample papers on the HMT website www.harris-meltzer-trust.org.uk.

D onald Meltzer frequently prefaces his accounts of Melanie Klein's role in the advancement of psychoanalysis by pointing out that she was not interested in being a theoretician but in following her insights as a clinician; although she was fiercely protective of her ideas when she knew what she could see.

In this light, *Richard Week-by-Week* represents a unique and innovative approach to teaching the insights and techniques of Kleinian psychoanalysis, with Mrs Klein herself as teacher and learner at the same time (Meltzer was fond of quoting Sylvester's dictum 'that teaching others, I myself may learn' – see his introduction). *The Narrative of a Child Analysis* offers a unique opportunity to watch Mrs Klein at work in the whitehot environment of the play-consulting room, pushing the boundaries of her conceptual tools whilst remaining acutely sensitive to the needs and sensibilities of the child and the transference emotions which are always at the forefront of her attention.

Richard's analysis, when aged ten, was time-limited to four months and took place in Scotland during wartime, which gave it a particular concentration as, like the idea of death, both partners worked under the shadow of an irrevocable termination – one of Richard's realistic anxieties being his awareness that Mrs Klein would be returning to the London of the Blitz. In addition to the pressurised context of the *Narrative*, there is a special intensity in Meltzer's critique that derives from the counterpoint of identifications. It constitutes an intimate dialogue with Mrs Klein, his own analyst, some fifteen years after his analysis had ended (at the time of her death), just as Mrs Klein in the book is reviewing her experience some fifteen years after the work with Richard had taken place. It is her testimony to the truth of the analytic experience and, like all autobiographical narratives, builds on the tension of 'I then, I now' (as Virginia Woolf put it). Meltzer, in his detailed critique and in analogous autobiographical vein, balancing his own child–mother relationship with Klein against his own personal experience of analysing children, points out to the reader the key moments of tension, revelation, and countertransference stress, and their significance in terms of both personality development and of psychoanalytic method. Through these 'aftersights' he clarifies for us the brilliance of Mrs Klein's technique and her capacity to encourage her patient's capacity for love whilst trying to judge the degree of intimacy that would be helpful and not counterproductive given the constrained circumstances. Long before the view of psychoanalysis as a communication between two minds became accepted currency, Mrs Klein demonstrates her willingness to modify her interpretations in the light of further observations and to work with the child, allowing him to make his own modifications and become a genuine co-operator in the analytic process, rather than 'working through' in the earlier sense of insisting on the patient's acceptance of an interpretation. But it is done without sentimentality and without succumbing to his (pathological) seductiveness, despite the countertransference temptation to make things easier for him owing to the imminence of separation.

During this personal journey alongside Mrs Klein and Richard, Meltzer highlights the genesis of her key contributions to psychoanalysis and their roots in (and deviance from) Freud: such as, her focus on emotionality rather than on impulse life, as it later came to be formalised in *Envy and Gratitude*; her knowledge (unavailable to Freud) of the mother-as-the-world of the young child and hence her different (more optimistic) view of natural curiosity despite its perversion by internal intrusive forces; the questions thereby raised about the multiple interactions of parts of the self with parts of objects, inside and outside, in the 'Russian doll' model; the necessary reinstatement in psychology of value systems in the new form of paranoid-schizoid and depressive positions. Above all perhaps, what is most fascinating is the evolution of her idea of the 'combined object', which crescendoes toward the end of her work with Richard, growing out of the Black Island dream (with its Wolf Man echoes), in the form of playing with her umbrella: 'The world which was turning round was the whole world he had taken into himself when he took the breast – or rather Mummy mixed with Daddy, and her children, and all she contained … That was also why he now treated Mrs K's umbrella more carefully than he had formerly treated Mummy's' – which Meltzer concludes is 'a gorgeous interpretation'. By the end of his brief but intense analysis Richard, says Meltzer, has found containment for his infantile fear of being dropped and can enter into his new status as 'a young man who knows that he needs analysis if he is going to develop properly and does not want to be a dunce.'

Meltzer's own love and admiration for Mrs Klein shines throughout his critique of the Richard story, making this probably his most personal and passionate book, a tribute to both his own analyst and to the analytic process.

Meg Harris Williams
(editor)

Any systematic attempt to teach Melanie Klein's work runs almost immediately into difficulties that are the exact opposite of the problems facing one in teaching Freud. Where the theoretical tail wags the clinical dog with him, hardly any theoretical tail exists to be wagged with her. This is not immediately apparent because all her earlier work (until the paper on manic-depressive states, but really only taking a clear-cut line of departure with the 1946 paper on schizoid mechanisms) is couched in the theoretical language of Freud and Abraham, shifting from the terms of libido and topographic theory to the new structural one.

One can hardly ascribe naiveté to such an astute woman; one must assume that the philosophy of science did not really interest her. The laws of evidence; the distinction between description, model, theory and notational system; the different classes of definitory statements – none of this concerned her. This was partly a matter of modesty, for she clearly considered her work to be merely a filling-out and clarification of Freud, and never recognized the huge leap she had made in method or model of the mind. She tended to be hurt and astonished by the hostility directed at her and thought of it only as antagonism to the ideas, much as Freud felt in his early isolation. But surely a great deal of this unfriendliness stemmed from very poor communication, linguistic snarls, further provoked by the dogmatic demeanour of her (and her colleagues') writing. These are the preconditions for political struggle over the 'mantle' – Freud's, Abraham's, later Mrs Klein's. Although it now becomes a bad pun to speak of dismantling the Kleinian myth, that is certainly one of the main functions of these lectures.

In order to do this I chose to re-enforce Mrs Klein's own courageous attempt, embodied in that unique and fairly unread masterpiece (Henry Reed said it stood beside *War and Peace* on his shelf), *Narrative of a Child Analysis*. On the whole the adventure has been successful in its lecture-seminar form. Whether this can be carried over into printed form is uncertain for two reasons; one is that the lectures are meant to be virtually unintelligible unless the actual text of the book has been studied carefully, or at least very recently read. The second reason is more complex. The lectures were impromptu (though carefully prepared), recorded and the text edited. The result is very unsatisfactory from the literary standpoint but has been retained because of the personal flavour of my relation to Mrs Klein (internally). It is hoped that in this way it would be possible to maintain a critical attitude side by side with admiration and respect without generating an atmosphere either of reverence or iconoclasm. My discussion of the clinical work has a background in an exhaustive study of the book made by a group (Esther Bick, Martha Harris, Doreen Weddell, Claude and Elinor Wedeles) in 1962–64 for which Dr Wedeles kept notes. But the criticisms and praise of Mrs Klein's work are totally my own responsibility.

So the first purpose of these lectures was to help people to read, preferably to study, this important book. The second was to use the clinical work and Mrs Klein's notes as basis for a semi-systematic review of her method and ideas. This stocktaking, since it is partly determined in its sequence by problems which arise in the clinical material, is not orderly either in an historic (or chronological) sense nor in a systematic one. Nonetheless many of Mrs Klein's important ideas are reviewed and brought into juxtaposition to Freud's, with some resultant clarification on both sides, I think.

Reading – works by Melanie Klein

(1930). The importance of symbol formation in the development of the ego. *International Journal of Psychoanalysis,* 11: 24–39.

(1932). *The Psychoanalysis of Children.* London: Hogarth.

(1935). A contribution to the psychogenesis of manic-depressive states. *International Journal of Psychoanalysis*, 16: 145–174.

(1937). *Love, Hate and Reparation* (with Joan Riviere). London: Hogarth.

(1940). Mourning and its relation to manic-depressive states. *International Journal of Psychoanalysis*, 21: 125–152.

(1945). The Oedipus complex in the light of early anxieties. *International Journal of Psychoanalysis*, 26: 11–33.

(1946). Notes on some schizoid mechanisms. *International Journal of Psychoanalysis*, 27: 99–110.

(1957). *Envy and Gratitude and Other Works.* London: Hogarth.

(1961). *Narrative of a Child Analysis.* London: Hogarth.

(1963). On the sense of loneliness. In: *Our Adult World and Other Essays.* London: Heinemann.

First week: sessions 1–6

Establishing the analytic situation; evolution of the concepts paranoid-schizoid and depressive positions

arrative of a Child Analysis seems to have been written between 1958 and 1960, after *Envy and Gratitude*, which appeared in 1957. The clinical work, done in 1941, was first written up in 'The Oedipus complex in the light of early anxieties' (1945) and then in 1946 came the paper which changed everything: 'Notes on some schizoid mechanisms'.

The first week of the analysis opens like a Chekhov play – immediately all the characters are introduced and all the themes and subplots are hinted at. An unlikely first week in the analysis of a ten-year-old. It is partly because Mrs Klein had already formulated some ideas in her mind, probably having taken a bit too much history from the mother. Consequently due to being in a hurry she makes mistakes which force things, mistakes in technique and interpretation which she has to make up for later. Her technique as she describes it in *The Psychoanalysis of Children*, was developed particularly with young children; and the technique with latency, pubertal and adolescent children was really an adaptation from this source. The basis of the technique aimed to establish the analytical situation, which meant getting some sort of transference going. Her way of getting it going was to perform some service to the child's unconscious by diminishing or modifying its deepest anxieties through interpretation.

Now Richard chronologically is a latency child, and you can see that when he comes to her, his manifest anxieties are at a minimum; whereas with small children her experience had always been that, in leaving the mother and coming to the play-room, the child would almost always experience severe persecutory anxieties which could be investigated with even minimal material. But with Richard it is quite different: there is very little manifest anxiety – she is not a doctor, she is not a man; he is quite used to charming and seducing women, and obviously has looked forward to seeing her. What can be seen happening in the first week is that, whether intentionally or not, Mrs Klein has set about mobilising anxieties, rather than diminishing them. And the technique she employs for mobilising Richard's anxieties is really no different from one for diminishing them: that is, to go right into the depths.

In the very first session she has done this in quite a masterful way, with the material about the fear of his mother being attacked by a tramp. Immediately the stage is filled with characters: the primal scene is introduced and the cast builds up through the next three sessions – there is mummy, daddy, brother Paul, Richard; there is Bobby the dog; somewhere there is 'Cook', Johnny Wilson, his analytical rival; and somewhere there is Mr Klein, who is not dead despite Richard knowing very well that he was, and there is Mrs Klein's son. And in the background of the stage set is the war situation with accomodating maps on the wall and all the other paraphernalia of the Girl Guides' room. In that sense it was a very unusual setting in which to practice analysis; indeed there seems to have been enough material scattered round the walls for one to deal with it almost like a Rorschach. Anything Richard might select could be taken as having associative significance for him because it was taken from such a tremendous array of pictures and postcards on the walls.

In the very first session one sees Mrs Klein forcing the situation: forcing it, for instance, in a way which she would generally have considered a technical error; that is, by using her knowledge of the history to seek a specific piece of material, namely whether he was worried about his mother. The material about the tramp immediately came out. She is nevertheless very gentle with Richard regarding aspects of his character which are in evidence, such as duplicity, trickiness and treachery – a theme which appears very early on. She never really confronts him with bad aspects of his feelings and impulses without immediately balancing it with a recognition of the other side – of his desire to preserve and protect.

In this first week, in addition to the creating or evoking of the whole setting of the child's life, Mrs Klein also unfolds for Richard a considerable panorama of her own theoretical equipment: the splitting of objects between good and bad, the conflict between love and hate, between persecutory and depressive feelings. She hints at mental mechanisms like the denial of psychic reality, the difference between wishing, thinking, doing; she suggests such things as splitting on to the dog parts of himself; she speaks about splitting within himself and delegating, for instance, a bad part of himself to the monkey; about the primal scene and phantasies of involving himself in it (the material about the two dogs with the little puppy between them). She unfolds theories concerning the oral, anal, and genital erogenous zones in relation to the dog Bobby eating coal and Richard wanting to play with his 'big job'; and finally she introduces him to the concept of omnipotence.

Now it seems to me that in many ways she introduces these concepts to him in a hurry, in ways that are a bit in advance of the material. This is most clearly seen with the introduction of the concept of omnipotence a propos the monkey and the concept of tragedy, and whether the tragedy was really that Richard caught cold or that he realized that his destructive impulses were too strong to control. But I think that in general one sees her operating in a way which she never describes yet which is quite important to recognize: she sets about (not just by giving him the name of sexual intercourse) building up and establishing a vocabulary and system of communication with him which was in many ways specific to the analysis, and in that way, private to the analysis. It was different from any way he had ever been talked to before. This aspect of her technique establishes a certain sequestration of the analytic situation. By mobilizing his anxieties and showing that there are means of communicating about them, that she has equipment for dealing with these anxieties and pains (even though he says he does not want to hear about such horrid things,) Mrs Klein very quickly and deftly constructs the situation. Within a week it can be seen that an analysis – and a very intense analysis – is going on. By the end of the week (when his mother has to bring him) he has a severe aggravation of his fear of children in anticipation of the weekend breaks, (quite unusual, for children do not usually anticipate the impact of the first weekend.) She has already afforded him a brief period of relief, indicated in the sixth session when Richard reported being able to play on the beach with a child and had lost his trowel. One of his main difficulties was his near total inability to socialize with other children.

So this is a very dynamic first week, with the analysis set going very rapidly, first, by specific mobilization of his anxieties through evoking his fears at night (the story of the tramp); second, by interpreting in a way which establishes the means of communication, for instance, about sexual intercourse (which no one had actually discussed with him before as an actual event between his parents, although his mother had given him 'information' about the 'facts of life' on several occasions); third, Mrs Klein then proceeds very quickly to investigate the phantasies and their implications and to draw them into the transference. She has set the situation going in spite of his consequent suspiciousness towards her (his fear of being trapped like the fleet in the Mediterranean, his fear of being abandoned like the soldiers in Crete); in spite of all these anxieties being mobilized and flooding him, she has afforded him a temporary relief which he could experience in an actual external situation. She has also achieved the arousal of curiosity and interest in her in the transference (shown by the questions about Mr Klein, his suspicions about her being Austrian, what countries she has visited). His playing with the clock and going into her bag, with the associations thrown up, are clear indications of infantile transference in this rather poised child.

All this is extremely impressive; and is in a way different from the notes she has given for the different sessions, which partly describe and partly apologize for the technique which she has used (for instance, in giving him so much information about herself, which she said she later regretted). Perhaps by implication she is also apologizing for being in a hurry with him. The only serious mistake which I think that she made is of the same order as the first one, about his worries for his mother, namely, bringing the material about his circumcision. This had really the opposite effect, coming later in the week, when the transference was already set going. The first question opened up the whole area of his fears at night and worries about his mother and protectiveness toward her, leading to Mrs Klein's being able to interpret that he felt he could protect her, thus denying his father's existence and the parents' sexual intercourse. It seems to me that when she made that mistake again, it had the opposite effect, of letting him off from a situation in which he was beginning to feel that she was getting a line on him about his duplicity, the violence in his nature, the biting, the anal preoccupations, the identification with the Hitler-daddy, the wish to get involved in the intercourse and make it into something bad. He was feeling that she was beginning to see that he was not a trustworthy ally for her or for anyone else; and somehow by raising this issue about the circumcision (for she was, it seems to me, interested in getting a little closer to castration anxiety) she lets him off. He begins to show her the scars of his operation and the tension goes out of the session. The preparation for the weekend goes adrift. Feelings of depression and anxiety that had been mobilized and led to his difficulty coming to the session, seem to melt away. These extremely dynamic and relieving five and a half sessions peter out at this point. It ends on a friendly note but in a rather low key.

In order to follow this massive clinical data of work done almost seventeen years before its publication, one must keep in mind where Mrs Klein was in the development of her thought and experience at the time of doing the clinical work, as opposed to writing the book. In the seventeen years between the two, there appeared such landmarks as 'Notes on some schizoid mechanisms', the paper on 'Loneliness', and the major work *Envy and Gratitude*. During this time her conception somehow mellowed and altered as a result of her forming a clearer idea about splitting processes – splitting of the self (for it was really only after 1946 that she began speaking consistently of the 'self ' rather than the 'ego', as being the structure that was split.) Although she never did clearly formulate the difference between the concepts of 'self 'and of 'ego', it is fairly clear that she meant it as a structure and not as 'self-representation' in the manner, say, of Jacobson.

I want to clarify the development of Mrs Klein's concepts of the paranoid-schizoid and depressive positions up to 1941 and subsequently. Her earliest writings were all focussed on the development of children with a very strong emphasis on the persecutory anxieties (which she also called paranoid anxieties). She repeatedly demonstrated that it was in the first two years of life, in pregenital development, that the fixation points for manic-depressive and schizophrenic illnesses existed. She asserted that children in the normal process of development went through phases of anxieties and phantasies characteristic of these mental illnesses. Later, she changed her mind in many ways about that, but her attitude in 1941 was that the phantasies and anxieties were identical, and that these illnesses were simply efflorescences and elaborations of the normal developmental experiences of children. This implied that the fixations were not, as Freud said, fixations of the libido, but fixations of the whole personality, including ego functions, superego constellations, and libidinal or id fixations. But at that time, she did not see that these illnesses had a special structure of their own; she saw them as developmental stages. It was on this ground that she was strongly attacked, for saying that babies were psychotic: and although she said she did not mean this, she did in fact say that babies were psychotic in ways essentially identical to schizophrenic and manic-depressive psychosis.

She was studying the functions that had begun during the earliest feeding period as she reconstructed it from psychoanalytical evidence with young children. She first placed the crucial development from part-object to whole-object relationships (following Abraham) at about six months, later moving it back to three months, marking the onset of the depressive position. Her idea was that processes of introjection and projection commenced at the very beginning of life, as soon as there was sufficient differentiation between self and object for an inner world to be built up. This is in many ways her least spoken about and perhaps greatest contribution to psychoanalysis – this development of a very concrete conception of the inner world. It has become that aspect of her work which most differentiates her followers from others in psychoanalysis. Her idea was, that from the very beginning, the experience of satisfaction, deprivation or disappointment resulted in the splitting of the object into good and bad, both of which were introjected. In 1946 she added that it was also the self that was split into good and bad; that the bad part of the self and the bad part of the objects became immediately fused into the major persecutor of the personality, which then had to be separated off and kept at a distance from the good or idealized parts of the self and objects, which in their turn also came together to form the core of the personality.

Thus her earliest work was preoccupied with the description of the severe persecutory or paranoid anxieties and the phantasies in which they were embodied, and the kinds of defences that were used by the infant and small child in relation to them. It was only in 1935 in the paper 'A contribution to the psychogenesis of manic-depressive states', that she began to talk about 'positions', a term which Fairbairn had already used, and I think she borrowed it from him. He had spoken of the 'schizoid position' and she spoke of the 'paranoid position'; later she fused the two into the 'paranoid-schizoid position'. While she felt that there was similarity with Fairbairn's views, there was also a difference. At the time when she first began to speak about positions, she did not only speak of 'paranoid position' but also of 'obsessive position' 'depressive position', and 'manic position'; and it is fairly clear that 'positions' first of all meant consortia of anxieties and defences. Thus her first idea of 'position' did not imply developmental significance, but pathological significance; it was not in any way a developmental phase, nor was it in itself a mental illness; it was a consortium or constellation of anxieties and defences and the impulses to which they related. She spoke of at least four positions to begin with. But by the time she wrote the paper on 'Mourning and its relation to manic-depressive states' (1938), she had reduced these to 'paranoid-schizoid position' and 'depressive position', not thinking of them as much as constellations of defences and anxieties, as manifestations of crucial attitudes towards the objects. This change from paranoid-schizoid attitudes to depressive attitudes toward the object was felt to be bound up very specifically with the transition from part-object to whole-object relations – that is, the beginning of seeing the object as whole, unique, irreplaceable, and no longer exchangeable for other part-objects. It was from this whole-object experience that concern, and what she called at this time 'pining' for the object, was felt to develop; and she felt that it manifested itself toward the end of the first year of life, specifically in relation to the comings and goings of, firstly, the breast and then the mother, as the breast-mother. Therefore at this point, she was talking of paranoid-schizoid position and depressive position as developmental phases and the fixation points for schizophrenia and manic-depressive psychosis respectively. But she had some difficulty in relating them to the developmental phases of the libido and the progression of the erogenous zones. She therefore speaks not of 'entry' into the depressive position but of 'overcoming' the depressive position. I take it that by 'overcoming' the depressive position she meant learning to tolerate the depressive anxieties about the destruction of the good object, and being able to bear separation from an external good object, on the basis of developing greater confidence in the security of the internal object. At this point the emphasis was very much on this as a developmental accomplishment, although she says many times that it is never complete and the struggle to establish it has to go on over and over again throughout life. This nodal accomplishment enables the child to establish internal security on the basis of which intellectual functions, symbol formation, socialization, the ability to relate to people other than the mother, the development of the Oedipus complex and relation to the father, both positive and negative, taking an interest in the other children in the family – were all dependent; and sublimations (of which she still speaks) also required this 'overcoming' of the depressive position. So at this time, what she seems to mean by 'overcoming' the depressive position is really this crescendo of pining anxiety: every time the child or baby was separated from its primary maternal object in the outside world, it was still vulnerable to attack from its persecutors because its internal object was not securely established. That seems to me to be the second stage in the development of the concept.

As the concept developed later (beyond the work with Richard) it was very different: Mrs Klein no longer spoke usually of 'overcoming' the depressive position, but rather of 'attaining' it, 'achieving' it, 'penetrating' it. She began to view it less as something to be accomplished than as something to be struggled toward with increasing mastery. It became something more like an area of life; so that the world of paranoid-schizoid object relations and the world of depressive relations were two different worlds which had a certain relation to internal and external but could be switched around: she speaks quite early of 'flight to internal objects' when external objects become persecutory, or 'flight to external objects' in manic denial of psychic reality when the internal objects are persecutory. So, as they later develop, 'paranoid-schizoid' and 'depressive positions' become areas of object relationships in which different value systems prevail, having neither any particular significance as developmental phases nor as psychopathological constellations. Their significance is rather that of economic principles – though she never came to any clear statement of it – which in a way transcended Freud's description of the pleasure principle modified by the reality principle. From the theoretical point of view, this is the main thing to keep in mind a propos the work with Richard: that Melanie Klein did this analytical work while thinking of the depressive position as something that had to be overcome, and whose main characteristic was separation anxiety – the pining for the good object. The elements in depressive anxiety connected with guilt, remorse and loneliness were satellites to the central position of pining in separation, consequent to omnipotent (masturbatory, usually) attacks on the internal object.

CHAPTER TWO

Second week: sessions 7–12

The developmental role of the thirst for knowledge

This second week is a marvellous week of analysis. I said the first week was like the opening of a Chekhov play with all the characters and the stage setting, Mrs Klein introducing her concepts and her language, and Richard being charming and getting frightened. Mrs Klein was in a hurry and unused to this setting, not knowing how to operate it. But the second week is entirely different, she hardly puts a foot wrong and things move on in the most astonishing way. If the first week sets the stage, the second week really introduces the drama and produces the first real formulation. I will try to describe it in phenomenological terms.

Richard's modes of representation become evident; the geography for instance. It becomes quite clear that the inside of the playroom is generally a very 'inside the mother's body' situation and that he has a tendency to escape to the outside to look at the hills. The exception to this is when he looks out of the window, which often seems to have the meaning of being outside looking in, and then he sees the children and the horse and so on. It is a common phenomenon with younger children. If you wear glasses, the child might come and look into you in the same way. Thus the geography of Richard's phantasy begins to come clear, inside and outside of objects. In the last session another type of geography closely related to conscious and unconscious is suggested. It is represented in the drawing of the ocean with the ship on top and the starfish and submarine and so on underneath. Mrs Klein suggests to him that this represents his desire to split these two levels. The division in the geography, of inside and outside in relation to the object, is thus paralleled by the geography of internal and external world in relation to himself. Likewise his splitting of the self begins to be evident. At least three divisions in his personality are fairly distinct; there is a really nasty, rather fascist and primarily oral sadistic part that bites his cap when he thinks about the ship's captain that he admires, or wants to burrow its way into Mrs Klein's mind, identified with the rats which used to be at his old school or in the laundry in X. It also has certain anal sadistic qualities that are connected with bombing and his preoccupation with 'big job', his laughing at the backside of the clock and laughing at the map when he looks at it upside down, or not liking the picture because it is brown. Secondly, there is a part of Richard which is affectionate and tender, that nuzzles the clock with his lips, that appreciates the beauty of the hills, likes the picture of the landscape, admires the tower and the sun shining on it. It obviously has a capacity for deep feeling but also utilizes these feelings in a very manic way, which Mrs Klein now notices. His relationship to beauty is attenuated by his manic use of it for the purpose of denying both the destructive feeling and the depressive anxiety about the damage that he may do. Finally Mrs Klein defines the sly, deceptive, seductive part of himself, the part that can easily change back and forth, that shows her how a Nazi flag can be changed into a Union Jack by just adding a couple of lines. Also his tendency to seek alliances emerges: with his brother, with his dog Bobby, with John Wilson. The wish for a sister and for other siblings as allies, both against the parents when they are bad and also against the destructive aspects of himself becomes a bit clearer.

Another category is the phenomena that begin to accumulate around the inside of the mother's body and its population, the representation of the father's penis in the electric bars of the fire that Richard turns on and off, the dirty children in the street, the girl with protruding teeth, the red haired girl, the wicked boy who was nasty to him, the little stools that he dusts so very vigorously and beats, and, in the drawings, the little starfish, which Mrs Klein at first interprets as the baby part of himself.

It comes out pretty clearly that Richard is a burrower-in and he tends to experience his closeness to Mrs Klein in the light of his intrusive voyeurism, a theoretical area we will return to shortly. The fact that she is not so seducible as the other women he has been accustomed to charm has the effect of drying up his chat so that he becomes more depressed and inhibited with her. In the last session of the week she introduces the drawing materials again which seems a bit surprising. She might have left it over till the next week but it was probably a part of her being in a hurry, feeling that he was drying up and getting slightly worried about what kind of weekend he would have.

Richard's curiosity seems to have the meaning of getting inside her. The inside of the room becomes very significant as the inside of her body, while the clock with its front side and backside suggest that the inside of the mother's body also has some structure corresponding to the external features of a front side and a back side, namely, a good clean place and a bad dirty place. Insofar as it is occupied by the objects of his jealousy (the daddy's penis, the babies, the little foot stools, the other children that use the room, her other patients) Richard becomes very confused about good and bad and consequently has much anxiety about food, whether it is good or if it might be spoiled in any way.

Mrs Klein does not link this confusion to another phenomenon that appears in the first three sessions, that is, Richard going to urinate. It is a bit surprising that she does not link it with the way in which the oven seems dirty and the ink smells bad, and the foot stools are dirty and have to be beaten to make them clean. But what she does pick up and render as a beautiful formulation is that he cannot attack the daddy's penis and the babies inside the mother as his enemies without endangering the mother. This comes out in the material about attacking Hitler inside France.

Mistakes of the first week such as leading him by asking about the circumcision and about his mother's illness are not repeated. Asking him if his father is bald is not quite in the same category. When she has hints from the material she feels free to seek information about the child's life situation that might confirm or refute its significance. She seems to have become more comfortable in the room despite the nonsense about the key. Her technique settles down as she becomes more relaxed in the setting and feels that she is beginning to grasp what kind of a human being Richard is, that he is very frightened, very tricky and sly, and that he is very split and different parts of himself know very little about one another. But she also sees that he is urgently wanting help, as when he questions her about whether she had trouble when she was a child. Mrs Klein sees that he is always on guard, it becomes quite clear that he is miserable and furthermore that he knows that he is miserable. In a sense she helps him to a greater awareness of it by scotching some of his more psychopathic seductiveness. Probably the impact of the first weekend has already deepened the transference, in spite of his claim that he had a lovely time and the tragedy was hurting his leg. But he subsequently hurt his leg again before the next session. Mrs Klein only takes up the theme of castration anxiety that she was following in the previous week, but she does do a lot of linking.

One can see that she is constantly correcting her interpretations, quite unashamedly. If her interpretation proves useless she sweeps it aside and replaces it or rebuilds it or reconstructs it. She is constantly gathering the material together, making lists of the phenomena that are connected, like the horse's head and Turkey on the map, the little stools and the fire. Now that she has started to do a lot of linking, gathering bits together, one really begins to see Mrs Klein at work and to see in the second week what a diligent analyst she was, how hard she worked for the children, the richness of her imagination, her capacity to use the material, and to conduct experimentation in thinking. She could throw things out and try new things to see if they fitted better.

This second week conveys the sense of the relaxation with which she worked, whereas in the first week she was tense and in a hurry and, in a sense, placating and overdoing the emphasis on Richard's good feelings. After a mere twelve sessions a real analysis is going and a first major formulation has been made as regards the depressive conflict, that is, that you cannot attack the inside of the mother containing your rivals and enemies, without harming the mother herself. She picks up the connection between the black car with all the number plates (which must have been old number plates, 'dead' number plates) representing dead babies and the way in which Richard plays with the electric fire noticing that something moves inside it when he switches it on and then it stops moving and goes black and dead-looking when he turns it off. This will turn out to be the central theme of the whole four months of work.

Richard's urge to get inside the mother, both to attack and find out if everything is all right, illustrates a key concept of Melanie Klein's work. It is an intrusive voyeurism which is looking for the dirt, laughs at the funny bottom and wants to beat the babies and bite the penis inside. But is is also an anxious, worried intrusiveness which wants to find out the truth about whether the mother is all right in spite of the attack. This is a differentiation which she does not really make clear anywhere in her writing although I think it is absolutely implicit in her clinical material. In her paper on 'The importance of symbol formation for the development of the ego' (1929), she wrote about a little boy named Dick who seemed very close to being autistic. She described beautifully how she got his treatment going but, what is more interesting, is the question she raises regarding symbol formation and how is it related to the thirst for knowledge or the epistemophilic instinct. When does it all start and how is it connected with the early stages of development? Freud's idea about curiosity did not in any way distinguish between curiosity and the thirst for knowledge. He linked it specifically to what he called the 'sexual researches of children' which he thought arose somewhere around three-and-a-half to four years of age when the Oedipus complex was set in motion. In his theory, the desire to know and understand was, at its foundation, the desire to know about the parental intercourse and in later writing was connected to the primal scene (the Wolf Man case). This desire to know about the sexual intercourse was in the service of the need to dispel castration anxiety. All other thirst for knowledge was in the nature of a sublimation of that quest and therefore Freud tended to assume that people who had a strong thirst for knowledge had never solved their Oedipus complex and were inhibited sexually. This was in keeping with his whole idea about sublimation. In the Leonardo paper he rather assumes that genius and sublimation of homosexuality are absolutely bound up together.

Mrs Klein, almost from the very beginning of her work, in her first paper on observation of the development of a child, came to the conclusion that the epistemophilic instinct occurs at a very early age in connection with the conception of the inside of the mother's body. The desire of the child to know about it is highest when the mother is still the 'world'. The curiosity about the mother's body extended naturally to curiosity about the child's own body and played a part in the formation and creation of an internal world. It also naturally extended itself through symbol formation on to other people, other people's bodies and minds and then to the whole world. It did not require a process of sublimation but only an extension through symbol formation, which was a search for meaning. Sublimation, on the other hand, is a means of manipulating the libidinal impulses in the service of defence against anxiety. That is a major philosophical difference between Mrs Klein's ideas about mental life and Freud's. He tended to look backwards through the lens of psychopathology whereas she looked forward through the lens of child development. In the late 1920s when she wrote the paper about Dick she thought that curiosity was, in the first instance, driven by the eruption of oral sadism. This, and the greed connected with it, linked with the conception of a combined object (although she does not at that time call it a combined object) – the father's penis inside the mother. It was this oedipal constellation that excited the baby's greed and its sadism and its wish to explore the contents of the mother's body.

That was her earliest formulation but it does not make any distinction between the possible difference of motives. That is, it docs not distinguish between the intrusion for destructive motives, the wish to know as a primary satisfaction, and the wish to know driven by depressive or persecutory anxiety. Of course, she had not then formulated the depressive position, but by the time she was doing the work with Richard, she had done so. What can be seen in the material of this second week and this first major formulation is at least dual motivation for the curiosity; one aspect is the rat-like burrowing in, wanting to steal, wanting to spoil, wanting to bite; the other is wanting to get in, wanting to find out if everything is all right. When he finds an envelope full of pictures, he counts them; this is clearly linked to the number plates of the car and the concern with the seven little stools. It is, in effect, a defect in the formulation that, although she calls it an epistemophilic instinct, she does not treat it as an instinct, but as a defensive reaction. It is not quite the same impulse as in Freud's view, but none the less it is represented as having to be driven by anxiety and must therefore derive its meaning from its relation to anxiety. Not until Bion's work does the thirst for knowledge find a truly primary role in mental functioning and development.

Third week: sessions 13–18

Envy and Gratitude as the organizing postscript to the body of Melanie Klein's theoretical work

This week is a most astonishing one, rushed forward very much by the fact of Richard's mother being ill, first of all from eating salmon and later with a sore throat. The fact that she disappoints him by not coming to 'X' with him and not visiting him, keeps the tension up and drives the depressive aspects into the forefront of the material in a very premature way. In that sense it is rather a misleading week and in a way it also misled Mrs Klein into overestimating Richard's capacity for depressive feeling.

It seems fairly clear that the coincidence of this with the material of the previous week when he started doing the drawings of the starfish and the submarines, and thus the coincidence of the revelation of his internal attacks on his objects with the external situation of his mother falling ill and the canaries going bald, really seems to have caught him in a kind of emotional vice that pushed him deep into hopelessness. It can be seen as a little depressive illness from which Mrs Klein extricated him with her interpretive work and enabled him to have depressive anxieties instead. The circumstances surrounding the secret that he defaecated in his pants and the way in which it was connected with the bombings and torpedo-ings quite overwhelmed him. In at least three sessions of the week one sees him, at least part of the time, quite depressively ill, absolutely joyless, unable to take an interest, not wanting to talk, or play, or draw ... not wanting to do anything. Mrs Klein does manage to pull him out of it very well.

The formulation, mainly centred on his jealousy, that, when he attacked the father's penis inside the mother as if it were a bad penis, he endangered his good object, the mother, undid Richard's pretence of protecting her from the tramp penis. This increased the fear that he would either destroy her or that his love for her would turn to hatred, as towards Germany, or that it would drive her into an alliance with the Hitler-father and thus turn her into an enemy. That formulation launches the analysis and galvanizes it into a going concern from the point of view not only of the development of the material but also the development of Richard's participation, intellectually and emotionally. It is a bit interfered with because the external factor that propels him towards depressive feelings and despair tends also to enhance his paranoid response. For instance he asked the cook what she thinks is going on at home and she replied that they were having a lovely time, and Richard exploded inside at the thought of it.

This brings out a very different picture from the formulation Mrs Klein had made to him the previous week about his jealousy. At this moment clearly the central problem is envy. In her formulations Mrs Klein swings back and forth between talking of his jealousy and talking of his envy and has not quite centred on the envy, perhaps because of a certain reluctance to do so. The fact that she only has a short time with him may influence her judgment. She may have thought, even in 1941, that a problem of integrating envy would not be greatly forwarded in a mere four months.

The main thing is to understand the development of material in this week because it is particularly interesting. She had rather hastened the emergence of the drawing activity on the Saturday and Richard rather dived into it and was a bit dismayed when he discovered that she could analyse his drawings. The same thing happens this week in the second session when he asks her to bring the toys back and he sees that she can analyse his playing with toys as well. There is no keeping secrets from her! Finally he tells her that he has a secret but can not reveal it. Just as he said he thought he could retain his faeces and failed, out comes the secret. At the end of the week he brings her a dream – final capitulation! There is no keeping anything from her. He is playing, he is drawing, he is telling her his dreams and associations – he is cooperating in every way, even confiding that his mother sometimes accuses him of giving her headaches. One sees in this week relatively little of his trickiness and dissimulation, even when they are talking about the aeroplane drawings. He is saying 'Oh yes … it could be this and this …' and she is saying 'Ah yes . .. but it could be that as well' and he says 'Yes … but how about this.' Mrs Klein takes this up, and probably correctly, as alternative formulations, all of which have a certain validity. Yes, he is the only one who survives, and, no, the good family survives, and then everyone is killed. She sees these all as phantasies underlying alternative states of mind coming in rapid succession and in a very unstable relationship to one another.

Quite unlike the previous week, there is only one touch of suspicion, when she has to end the Thursday session a little early, and he asks her if she is going to see John a little earlier than usual. But otherwise Richard is in a much more trusting and much more dependent relationship to her, partly because he is in such trouble with his feelings towards his family, his mother in particular and anxiety about her illness. So that when he says he is so fond of Mrs Klein and she is so sweet, it seems to come through much more sincerely, even though one can see that it is a hedge against feeling anxious and persecuted by her or that she might desert him.

The drawings, as you can see, have already taken on the form that will characterize them throughout the four months. The Empire drawings have their beginnings in the very first drawing of a big starfish (number nine) with all the squares filled in with different colours and then surrounded by a line and filled in in red. Mrs Klein links this back with the fish in the drawing two days earlier, when he had represented a mother fish who had eaten a baby starfish which was making her bleed by cutting and rasping a hole in her side. The empire drawings, the undersea drawings, the aeroplane drawings and later on some train drawings more or less embrace the main themes, varied in minute ways.

When he starts to play with the toys the main themes of his play immediately come up; parental intercourse and the child watching them comes out repeatedly; there are representations of a more part-object relationship with the trains coming into stations and knocking buildings over; the theme of childrens' rivalry with the parents, (the little girls and the dog; the children going to Dover, etc.). And then, of course, there is the central theme of the catastrophe that he cannot prevent. Mrs Klein is very sensitive to the relationship of children to the play materials, apologizing for giving Richard two lorries that were rather too definitive in their function, one carrying coal and the other timber. She is also very sensitive to the childrens' feelings about their lack of mastery over the toys, and mentions how children are dismayed by their difficulty in painting, and how they cannot keep from making a mess, which distresses them. This is a bit true of the toys she has given Richard which tend to fall over; the woman falls off the swing, the buildings fall over, the minister and pink lady fall off the roof. He can not really impose his will upon them partly because they themselves are very unstable, and partly because his own dexterity is inadequate. She is very much aware of the way in which this can have an upsetting and oppressive effect on a child and probably can generate play disruption. Each successive time that Richard plays with the toys a disaster occurs and play is disrupted. He then either begins to draw or he becomes listless and wanders away. Mrs Klein recognizes that the play disruptions have something to do with the way in which the toys, by their own qualities, bring him into contact with his inability to keep things under control inside himself and in particular that he can not control his own destructive impulses. On the other hand, the train running amok and knocking everything over is mainly precipitated by the accident of the minister and pink lady falling off the roof.

It is probably a prejudice based on her work with younger children that the toys allow them somehow to experience the emotionality more vividly than by talking, drawing or even telling dreams. A modification of the formulation she had made to him the previous week now results. She sees in this assemblage (the play with the toys, the drawings and his relationship to her, all in the context of his mother's illness) a clear indication of envy, having to do with his feeling himself the outsider looking in upon his happy family consisting of his father, mother, Paul and the dog. It puts him in 'a blazing fury' as he says of the drawing about the octopus, or 'wild' as he describes the starfish in a later drawing. He is a child who suffers quite a lot from envy of other people's happiness and the happiness of their relationship; the closest he comes to one is quickly spoiled by his seductiveness, his omnipotence, his manic tendencies and his sexual excitement. His relationships end up in a disastrous way, just as the play with the toys ends up in disasters.

Mrs Klein begins to formulate to Richard now in this week that he really can not bear to see the happiness of the relationship of the good ones to one another, whether good ones consist of the father and mother in a good intercourse, or good babies inside the mother in a happy relationship, or good babies coming to the breast, or parents proud of their children. There is an envy of the goodness itself that wants to spoil it; not just to have it but to spoil it. It is this spoiling that she begins to see as an important feature of Richard's illness in this week.

As regards technique, this week is fairly flawless. A few times she seems to ask him questions that are a little beside the point ('Where did you get the gun? Whose gun was it?'). This is not really a good technique with Richard because any lead like that immediately produces material that has a fairly low order of validity. She makes some long interpretations to him. In spite of what she says in the introduction, it must be true that these interpretations, which are all gathered together and make up three quarters of a page, may have been interspersed bit by bit as the material was being produced. But it is not necessarily so, because she does at the end of the session often comment on how he behaved while she was interpreting. The impression is conveyed that, when she started, there was a certain suspending of action. He either listened or did not listen but did not do much else.

Perhaps she did make some very long interpretations to him in this week when she was under some considerable pressure to help him because of his severe distress. She realized that he was in a very despairing state about his mother's illness and could not get it in proportion in his mind. He clearly felt that something terrible was happening to her, all mixed up in his mind with the drawings of the submarines, the sinking of the Emden, the fish with the dreadful starfish baby inside her, rasping her open and making her bleed. Mrs Klein was in a very urgent state to give him some relief, but, oddly enough, not by drawing it into the transference, but by formulating it and giving him some insight into it. It does give him relief, at least from the point of view of helping him to get out of the feeling of being frozen by depressive illness and despair into being in contact with depressive anxiety and feeling ashamed and worried about himself and the problem of controlling his impulses.

In general, her way of working emerges clearly. She really meanders about in the material, formulating bits and pieces of it as she goes along, gradually, until something begins to come clear to her. Then she goes in more definitively and begins to formulate conflict and the structure underlying the conflict. Many of the things she says to Richard appear irrelevant, inimical to one another, or mutually exclusive. It is apparently a fairly true picture of how she worked, unashamedly in the dark, by serial approximation.

Although envy and jealousy are not yet clearly differentiated in the clinical work with Richard, one can see the germ of the eventual book, *Envy and Gratitude*. The skeletal paper for this book was read at the 1957 Congress and it appeared in the following winter. It was the link that bound her work together, made it an integrated structure and set it on a different course from Freud's. In it she clearly distinguished between envy and jealousy, gave envy its correct status in relation to splitting processes, the therapeutic process, the negative therapeutic reaction and its relation to the future of psychoanalysis. This book stands in an interesting juxtaposition to Freud's 'Analysis terminable and interminable'. Just as that was a valid but gloomy document in relation to psychoanalysis, this book seems to me to be an incredibly hopeful one. Both focus on the negative therapeutic reaction. Whereas Freud's pessimism stemmed from his loyalty to the libido theory, feeling that in the final result everything was a matter of mental economics, of forces impinging on the ego, balanced against one another, ultimately the life and death instincts, Mrs Klein acknowledged the constitutional factors in relation to envy and does consider it to be one of the main manifestations of the operation of the death instinct upon the ego. But what she emphasized was a structural viewpoint, namely that the role of envy in the personality depends less on quality of virulence or quantity of intensity than upon its location and distribution. In this book she talks about splitting processes and the differences between excessive or inadequate splitting on the one hand, or inadequate splitting-and-idealization on the other. Primal splitting-and-idealization has to be just right so that goodness and badness of self and objects are adequately separated from one another, but not so widely separated that they cannot be brought into any kind of contact. The good self and the idealized object need to have a snug little time with one another until they get strong enough to admit the badness a little bit into their association. That model of the developmental process and the role of splitting-and-idealization and subsequent integration of the destructive envy made it possible to imagine that the envy might not merely be controlled but even ameliorated in its virulence.

Mrs Klein's advances in the concepts of splitting mechanisms and the nature of narcissistic identifications gave a new substance to Freud's structural concepts and brought them into the consulting room. The analyst could now begin to study not just in terms of the ego, the id and superego but also the bits and pieces of the personality and the bits and pieces of the objects to which they were related. The concept of projective identification made it possible to study just what we are beginning to see here with Richard, that is the inside of himself projected outside himself. By introducing the concept of envy and distinguishing it from jealousy, Mrs Klein started an important development in psychoanalysis, of finding words with which to dissect emotions just as she had earlier begun to differentiate different qualities of mental pain, persecutory and depressive.

Fourth week: sessions 19–24

Unconscious phantasies as mechanisms of defence, with special reference to obsessional mechanisms

This fourth week of analysis is also rather a splendid one and raises some interesting theoretical problems regarding obsessionality. The question of obsessional mechanisms is a puzzling and difficult aspect of Mrs Klein's work, since it is nowhere particularly set out. This is a week again punctuated by a disturbance in the setting. The mother's illness interfered in the third week. This week, in the second session, Mrs Klein has to take him to her lodgings and this also interferes in some way, although it is not so clear how and she takes it up very little.

The analysis is already going quite smoothly; she is working very confidently with him, sorting things out and throwing things away, and turning up new ideas. The changes in the formulation are changes in her ideas and attitude about the meaning of the material, but a lot of it has to be attributed to the deepening of the transference relationship so that it is more clearly differentiated from Richard's relationships at home to his parents, brother and Bobby. This is reflected very clearly in the way Mrs Klein interprets to him. The mode of presentation of the material keeps changing; he brings the fleet and then he draws, he plays with the toys and squeezes the football, he wanders about the room.

In between he talks to Mrs Klein, confiding in her little things John said (that he wished she were dead), telling her a dream in the fourth session and being very confiding also about the paranoid suspicions about her. These are now becoming much more intense because they are also juxtaposed to the building up of a much more genuine positive transference. One still feels Richard to be disingenuous at times. It mainly comes out with regard to the drawing, when he starts saying why there are two of this and three of that, or one of the other. His sincerity is not so convincing but most of the time he works closely with her. Anecdotal material from his life outside the consulting room begins to enter, like the business of whether he could stay in the cinema in the evening or whether he had to run out because he felt sick from the noises of the sing-song. Altogether, as far as material is concerned, there are hardly any doldrums. Richard seems most of the time to pay attention to what Mrs Klein says, even when he is suspicious and is questioning how she can know what goes on in his mind. She explains to him how she works and examines the material, what it may mean about his unconscious and so on. Even at times when there is great suspicion and doubt he is really working with her. It is rather a joy to see this sort of thing from a little boy who seems to be able to tolerate very little in the way of discomfort. Yet, when it comes to mental pain he is not too bad about it. He does soldier on somehow, better than one would perhaps have expected in the first couple of weeks.

The fleet material is of particular interest, probably partly because he brings it in himself and with his precious ships he does represent things that are different from his play with Mrs Klein's toys. The fleet play bears more on the organization of his family and the attempt to weld it together harmoniously, so that there would not be outbreaks of violence and chaotic running amok, whereas with the toys and trains all hell is let loose as soon as masturbation is represented by the swing in motion or the dog wagging its tail. With the fleet Richard is somehow trying to construct an idea of the possibility of a family where things are balanced, equal. No one should be saying I'm more important than you are. Paul need not be grabbed by Cook and Bessie because he is screaming and yelling that Mummy is with Richard, nor are the children engaged in homosexual activities because they are so furious about mummy and daddy being together.

All these different situations that disrupt the harmony of the family are rather beautifully represented in the fleet play, perhaps in a more convincing way than the drawings of the submarines, fishes and starfishes. This may be due to the equivocal quality of the drawings like that little argument about whether the torpedo was going to hit the ship or not. Somehow with the fleet he is more in control and can manoeuvre the relationships and represent them more accurately. Mrs Klein describes what emerges as obsessional mechanisms. Richard attempts through the fleet play to figure out a method of carefully balancing the privileges, pains and pleasures of each member of the family in such a way that harmony reigns and all the enemies are outside the family. This is a very important part of the obsessional mechanism, the attempt to achieve stability by balancing. But it is also very clear that to effect this balancing another technique is also required, omnipotent control and separation. It comes out particularly when he manoeuvres Rodney and Nelson to represent the daddy courting the mummy, very gently (not quite touching). These two mechanisms, the attempt to achieve a balanced situation and to effect it through omnipotent control and separation of the objects are described by Mrs Klein in the notes to this week and are probably her most advanced statement about obsessional mechanisms. She has used the term many times and in many different ways throughout her writing.

These obsessional mechanisms would, if they succeeded, enable Richard to establish a latency period in the ordinary sense. But it is also fairly clear that he is not able to stabilize things, partly because Mrs Klein is interfering by interpretation, but one also feels that he is not really able to manage the violence of his impulses by mechanisms of this obsessional sort. Instead what happens is that the material of the analysis begins to deepen into what one would call more psychotic levels that require a rather different formulation from those Mrs Klein found herself making in the first three weeks. There, after all, she was, in one way or another, interpreting first his castration anxiety in relation to his Oedipus complex, then something more related to obsessional despotism and conflict between love and hate with envy and jealousy coming into it, all on a rather whole-object level, not very much connected with projective identification or with part-object relations.

This kind of formulation would imply ordinary neurotic difficulties, that his fear of the other children might be connected mainly with his jealousy of his sibling, Paul. In the first three weeks there was abundant evidence of claustrophobic anxiety and of phantasies related to projective identification. The drawing of the fish with the starfish inside it, making a hole and causing it to bleed; the material about the Mediterranean with ships being trapped there, or troops being trapped on Crete, or his going out of the playroom: all these bits of evidence of claustrophobic anxiety were not quite in the forefront of the material. But in this fourth week, as a result of Mrs Klein interpreting to him the attempts to establish a quietus in his internal situation by means of these obsessional mechanisms of omnipotent control, separation and balancing, and thus disabling him, so to speak, from establishing this somewhat phoney quietus, the material deepens.

First of all clear material marks the emergence of his homosexuality on an oral level referable to preoccupation about sucking the penis and his playing games in bed with Bobby. Then there is the marvellous dream about the fishes. In a way it seems that Mrs Klein does not make as much of that dream as she might, mainly because she does not relate it to the drawing where the starfish were in a rage and were pulling the octopus out from where it was hiding and eating the grass. She recognizes the octopus as the father's penis inside the mummy, being attacked by these greedy babies who wanted to have the mummy all to themselves. But for some reason she does not interpret the fishes that invited Richard to dinner, and particularly the very insinuating and ingratiating manner of the chief fish, in a way that connects with the homosexual material that has just come previously, about Bobby and about Richard sleeping in Paul's bed. Have the fishes invited Richard to join them in devouring the father's penis inside the mother, or do they intend to devour Richard when he is in projective identification with this penis? Mrs Klein interprets it in terms of a claustrophobic anxiety, a fear of being trapped, as she had interpreted before the evidences of claustrophobia in relation to herself and the room, or like the ball he wanted to get out of the cupboard. Her work with this dream is not quite as powerful as it might have been, had she linked it to the homosexual material and the evidences of a collusive alliance with Paul or Bobby against the parents and their heterosexuality. It would thus have lent itself to connection with his identification with Hitler in the material in which he tells the boy to go away and gives the Hitler salute and later stamps up and down and goosesteps. The gang would eat up the father's penis and in that way assimilate its power and take over the world. What she does emphasize, however, is the theme of betrayal when he flees from the fire leaving his family behind. Richard is very uneasy about this interpretation and confabulates an addendum to the dream in which he puts out the fire and restores the fertility of the ground that has been scorched.

The theme which will become the main focus of the analysis begins to be represented this week by the Empire drawings. These are an elaboration of the starfish drawings and particularly the multi-coloured one in the red circle (No. 9). It links also with that picture of the fish containing the starfish, (No. 7) and touches on a very important theoretical problem that must have been exercising Mrs Klein at the time of the treatment, namely the interplay of projection and introjection, and of the identification processes they set in motion. By the time she was writing the book and the notes, she was tremendously interested in problems of structure: if a part of the self was put into an object, was it ego or was it self? did it in itself have internal objects? were those objects the same as the internal objects of other parts? if this was projective identification with an internal object, how could that have internal objects? She found herself elaborating some kind of Russian doll model of the mind.

The other part of the material which begins to develop now is the squeezing of the football which goes through various stages accompanied by cock-and-hen noises and phantasies. As the empire drawings relate more to processes of rivalry for the external mother, the football material and its later elaboration as the 'baby-tank' relates more to Richard's experience of internal objects, and thus connects with his hypochondria. For instance, the phantasy that the egg is laid as the chicken's neck is wrung, is connected with anxieties about birth and Richard acknowledges that birth can be dangerous and painful to women, as his mother had told him. But in his phantasy it is connected with his concept of a sadistic penis, that goes in and does damage inside the mummy. On the other hand, the mother and the penis can come together to form the 'wicked-brute' object. The clarification and differentiation of the transference situation from his relationship to his mother brings out Richard's ambivalence to Mrs Klein, or rather his split relationship to her, to the 'sweet' Mrs Klein for whom he evidently does begin to feel some love, and the Austrian Mrs Klein who has the dead Mr Klein's penis inside her and is terrifically mistrusted. He wants to know whether they were on the other side in the previous war and asks her to read some 'Austrian' to him: he does not want to call it 'German'. As a result of that clarification of the transference and differentiation of it, and because she blocks his attempt to balance with obsessional mechanisms, the material deepens and the claustrophobic material begins to come forward. It is highlighted by the dream of being invited underwater to have dinner with the fishes, and is made current by his being unable to stay at the cinema because of his fear of the children there, of their attacking him. This is amplified by his questions to Mrs Klein about whether the big boys would hurt him if he went to boarding school.

This deepening of the material, with its preoccupation with the inside of the mother's body, his desire to penetrate into it, the greed for what it is felt to contain, the feeling that the father's penis is in possession and has to be eliminated somehow, all has the structure of a much more psychotic level of anxiety and preoccupation than she had been dealing with in the first three weeks.

A word should be said about the impact in this week of Mrs Klein seeing Richard in her room. Of course, at first he was quite excited and this seems to lead on to the feeling of being admitted, as it were, to the club. Now he is one of the select that comes to her room and therefore he is one of her men. Since she does not have intercourse with him she probably does not have intercourse with anybody and therefore everybody is equal: a happy analytical family. On the other hand, he is also very evidently disappointed, as when he scolds her a bit at the end of the Wednesday session for having left the window open previously. It gives impetus in one direction to the obsessional mechanism because he has been admitted to the intimacy of her rooms, but it also gives some thrust to the more paranoid feeling of being tricked, seduced, enticed. In that way it has a relation to the fish dream and the feeling of being invited in order to be devoured or in order to be lured into some bad alliance against his good object.

So much for the material of the week. Regarding the theory of obsessionality, a large conceptual difference from Freud's use of it must be noted. It has never been made very explicit anywhere in the literature although it has obviously caused terrific confusion and agitation all round. Freud's conception of defence really starts from two points: one is his recognizing repression as it operated in hysteria, in amnesias, in slips of the tongue and parapraxes and the ordinary amnesia for early childhood. But the concept of mechanism has another root in the formulation of the dream work, that is, the work done by the dreamer to change the latent content into its manifest content for the purpose of evading censorship. The latent content has been given a twist by logical or linguistic techniques such as condensation, displacement, reversal. In this way the dream work, in so far as it is equivalent to mechanisms of defence, consists of manipulation of the meaningful content of the latent dream. But when Freud talks about mechanisms of defence starting with repression, and then later adds further mechanisms such as projections, introjections, withdrawal of libido, introversion of libido and sublimation, then he is not talking about mechanisms operationally but rather phenomenologically. He is gathering under the rubric of repression all those phenomena which he thinks must be caused by some neurophysiological mechanism, the working of which he does not know. 'Repression' in that sense is truly mechanical. The sense in which Mrs Klein spoke of projective identification or splitting, as mechanisms was purely operational, and therefore merely a description of the unconscious phantasy, like Freud's description of dream work. The reason for Freud's use of the term was his dedication to the libido theory and to the concepts of the manipulation of quantities of excitation. Mrs Klein's work from the very beginning was bound to unconscious phantasy and its content. Therefore in her work the unconscious phantasy is the defence against anxiety.

Early in her work, Mrs Klein tended to use the term 'obsessional mechanism' as Freud had used it, phenomenologically. He spoke of obsessional mechanisms being in operation whenever obsessional phenomena were in evidence, as for instance in the Rat Man case. She recognized as early as *The Psychoanalysis of Children* that obsessionality had something to do with controlling other people or controlling the objects. A brilliant footnote links it with catatonia, as perhaps the ultimate in the sadistic employment of obsessional defence.

The other great difference between Mrs Klein's use of the term 'mechanisms of defence' and Freud's use of it lies in his contention that particular mechanisms of defence were very specifically related to what he called the problem of the 'choice of neurosis'. Now Mrs Klein seems not to have thought that, or, in a sense, to have neglected this aspect of Freud's work, partly because of moving the whole Oedipus complex back into early childhood in relation to part-objects, and partly because of having a more developmental view rather than psychopathological view of things. It was her idea that a mechanism of defence could be utilized at different stages of development in relation to different developmental problems and would therefore have different consequences depending on what sort of conflict it was deployed against. She also had the idea that a particular mechanism could be deployed on a spectrum varying from the most sadistic employment of it to the most sparing or even reparative use. In this sense, of longitudinal application and of variable spectrum of sadism, she developed the concept of obsessional mechanisms in a flexible and powerful way in relation to clinical phenomena.

If one turns to the instance here in Richard's fleet material, one can see that Mrs Klein thinks he is employing the obsessional mechanism, which she defines quite clearly as attempting to achieve a kind of balance through omnipotently controlling and separating, and that he is using it in relatively gentle and tender ways. It is an attempt to establish a quietus, a sort of *Pax Romana*, you might say, in which, under his benevolent despotism, everyone will be equal and happy. And that would be a very benevolent use of it, bordering on manically reparative use, of obsessional mechanisms, and it would typify the way in which these are generally used by children in the establishment of a more or less healthy latency period. But she also sees that Richard tends to employ the same mechanisms in a much more sadistic way, that is, a bit earlier when he attempts to keep everything motionless. This of course is more sadistic and its ultimate extrapolation would be to the motionlessness of suspended animation that is imposed upon objects in catatonia. It will come again towards the end in the 'Black Island' dream (85th session). Her most comprehensive description of obsessional mechanisms is to be found in the paper 'Mourning and its relation to manic-depressive states', but it is also a very confusing paper.

Fifth week: sessions 25–29

The anxieties of the paranoid-schizoid position: paranoid anxiety, persecutory anxiety, persecutory depression

This week of the *Narrative* is an important one and brings up some very interesting problems, giving us the opportunity to investigate the history of the paranoid-schizoid position. It is again a week that has certain outside interferences. The mother is ill again and she goes home to visit Paul, while the nurse comes to look after Richard. He is furious about it, and by the end of the week he is ill himself and misses the Saturday session, and the next three sessions up to Thursday of the following week. it is a week in which his seductiveness and his placation and his trickiness are fairly in abeyance. Instead, what emerges is something very paranoid in the boy. In the context of much greater co-operation with Mrs Klein, he is able to admit to her something that must have been quite unknown, not only to Mrs Klein, but to his mother as well, absolutely secret, namely his paranoid fears of being poisoned by Cook and Bessie.

The material develops on the heels of the previous week's work, with its extremely valuable dream about the fishes inviting Richard to dinner. Somehow the tension was lost a bit toward the end with the empire drawings. But he returns this week more deeply involved in the transference, although Mrs Klein's technique does not quite take into account the increased engagement. She is still inclined to relate the material back to his mother and father and Paul and not to acknowledge its gathering towards herself. This gathering and intensification partly results from her planned trip to London hanging as a threat over the sessions. She has not given him a date yet. In contrast, his mother's illness seems to have very little impact on the material in spite of that little dream in which Richard is having his throat operated on three times.

What impact his mother's illness does have, along with her going back home to see Paul, is switched quickly to compound an increasing preoccupation with Mrs Klein, the danger of her being bombed, her relationships with John, and her son, and the dead-but-alive Mr Klein. Richard now discovers that there is also somebody living at her lodgings with whom she might have dinner, the 'Grumpy Old Man'. The intensity of the jealousy is very much gathered together in the transference and the material plunges into far more part-object relations and far more primitive emotionality. This comes out very forcibly in his behaviour, gnashing his teeth, being very defiant towards Mrs Klein, muttering things against her, squirting water at her, throwing the pencil shavings at her, saying he was going to leave the room if he wished. But his feelings of resentment come out, also, because they are less under the sway of his omnipotence and can emerge in a more straightforward way in the transference. The result is that Richard can also be more confiding with Mrs Klein. It is in this context that he confides to her his fear of being poisoned, after she had picked up in a very astute way his distrust of her in the little incident about the Fifth Columnists and its addendum, the problem of confidentiality in the analysis.

Richard himself seems to experience this symptom as pretty mad. But he confides to her that he has had the delusion that Cook and Bessie were spies, that he has spied on them and listened to see if they were talking German, that he smelled the condiment bottles to see if they smelled like poison. This must also be connected with the question of the smell of ether versus the perfume his mother gave him to take to his tonsilectomy. His primitive reliance on the sense of smell is indeed very closely connected with paranoia and the use of non-social cues for making social judgment. The paranoic characteristically uses as evidence things other people would never consider to be evidence: the use of senses rather individually and rather omnisciently to pick out social cues.

This is the sort of thing Richard seems to acknowledge to Mrs Klein at this point, that he has used his ears and eyes and nose in this rather paranoid way, trying to determine whether Cook and Bessie were spies and then whether they were out to poison him. In the first session of the week he had mentioned the three children that made their mother sick on the tram or bus, and Mrs Klein connected this with his feeling that he was such a nuisance with his questions and his nagging that he was making his mother ill, and might do the same to Mrs Klein.

Several threads of material become tightly interwoven at this point to form the background of the paranoia. First there is the jealousy material already mentioned, along with the empire drawing where the three men, Daddy, Paul, and Richard, grab all the best territory and leave the mother with very little. Second, there is the noxious, invasive nuisance material which implies that the Mummy or Mrs Klein would wish to be rid of him. Finally there is the contamination material about the dirty water; how it gets dirty and how the water goes out of the sink and flows out of the pipe to the outside. It is all this that seems to be split off and projected into the bottle of poison that Cook and Bessie, who are in with German spies, would use to poison him and get rid of him because he is such a nuisance.

It is in effect a transformation of the earlier formulation Mrs Klein had made about the parents joined in intercourse against Richard. In this context of awareness of being a noxious baby with his nagging, his urine, his faeces, his continual questions and probing voyeurism, that the projection of that noxious quality on to the mother, really on to the breasts, represented by Cook and Bessie, generates his paranoia towards the breasts and the fear of being poisoned. There is also arising now in the material the theme about the dead baby. It emerges in the material about the sinking of the Hood, where Richard murmurs to himself under his breath 'Richard ... Richard ... Richard ...', later 'Daddy ... Daddy ... Daddy ...', and Mrs Klein so intuitively interprets to him that these were the drowning sailors calling for help. In the next session Richard was able to consider very seriously whether he would have been able to rescue all of them, or any of them, or whether he would have needed to be rescued himself and would have joined the others in calling for the daddy. In conjunction with this dead-baby and the drowning-baby material we also learn of Richard having an irrational fear of ghosts and of his nocturnal anxieties, for which he reports that his nurse or nanny used to have to sit up with him when he screamed in the middle of the night.

In a way Mrs Klein tried to relate these two bodies of anxiety, the persecutory anxiety, related to the dead baby turned into ghosts which would attack him in the night, and the paranoid anxiety about the breasts that had turned poisonous and had turned against him in alliance with the bad penis and were going to poison him. At this point of the analysis she is not able to separate them from a third situation, the anxiety that he himself might poison the breasts with his noxious urine and faeces, his insidiousness and trickiness. Mrs Klein was beginning to erect three different formulations, whose relationship to one another is not at all clear. It is not clear partly because Mrs Klein did not have a clear theoretical basis for distinguishing them. One is this severe anxiety about dead objects and ghosts, perhaps the most severe of the persecutory anxieties. The second is a moderately severe persecutory anxiety which is more in the nature of a suspension of trust in the goodness of the object. When there have been sadistic attacks upon the breast, particularly if these attacks have been made out of possessiveness of the breast and a wish to spoil it and poison it so that others can not enjoy it, there follows a reflux of anxiety that the subject has poisoned the breast for himself as well. These two persecutory anxieties can be discerned and in some way in between them is this other anxiety that has a resemblance to them but is also different in a way that is not at all clear at this point, paranoid anxiety.

Paranoid anxiety is not just a suspension of trust in the good ness of the object; its core is a really severe confusion between what the paranoid feels and what he thinks. In his feelings he is drawn to the attractiveness of the object: in his thoughts he is frightened of its malevolent core. And this is the situation that is presented about Cook and Bessie. Quite clearly the two of them also represent part-objects. Here Mrs Klein makes the clearest formulation anywhere in her work about the nature of the combined object at part-object level, that is, the penis in the breast. This combined breast and nipple somehow creates confusion between good and bad. The division between feeling attracted to the breast and thinking that the nipple is not to be trusted creates the atmosphere of paranoid anxiety. The Thursday starts as a very defiant session and ends quite tenderly with Richard admiring the scenery, going out because he cannot bear the playroom at this point, feeling it to be a horrible, filthy place. He admires the hills and talks about climbing them with Mrs Klein. I think she lets him off quite a bit when she interprets his digging the stick into the ground as some sort of reparative intercourse. By the Thursday session he must have already been a bit ill. He did not come for the Friday session and went home till the following Thursday.

In the beginning of her work Mrs Klein used paranoid and persecutory as synonyms. Here in talking about Richard she does not make a clear distinction between them although later on in the book she does clarify this. Now the point is that in her very earliest work she described an essentially biologically determined efflorescence of sadistic impulses in the baby toward the breasts, attacking them in fact and phantasy, primarily out of greed, perhaps a little out of envy, but mainly out of greed. The modes of attacks were essentially biting and scooping, which were intended to rob the breasts, as part-object, of their food, and when extended to the mother as a whole object, to rob her of her beauty, food, babies and internal penises. But the earliest was the part-object relationship to the breasts, scooping them out in the greed to possess the food and to have absolute access to the breasts at any given time. The anxieties which this produced followed the Law of Talion – what you do to the breasts, they will then do to you: a logical operation, very much in keeping with Freud's views about how love turned to hate. Mrs Klein at this time, was also thinking mainly in terms of logical operation, but as her work developed it became clear to her that the child was persecuted by the damaged object. That was during the early 1920s and she did not find a solution to this problem of why the damaged object was a persecutor until 1957 when she discovered that the damaged object was felt to be envious of the intactness of other objects or the self. Many of the attacks which were earlier described as sadistic, biting, cutting, tearing, and so on, could be later seen to be attacks by projective identification. This made a very big difference in her views, that it was not simply 'if you're nasty to me, I'll be nasty to you'. The mental operations were much more complicated when the attack was in a concrete form and that the biting or scratching or spitting or urinating merely implemented the mental mechanism of projective identification. An object was wounded essentially by thrusting into it a part of the self which was in pain and contained vicious or destructive impulses. By this projection, the object then took on the malevolent characteristics.

As a consequence, Mrs Klein was very inclined to think of internal persecution as being equivalent to hypochondria and spoke about persecutory hypochondria and depressive hypochondria. Although in a sense this is a simple view of hypochondria, it was nonetheless an advance over Freud's work. His most developed idea was that hypochondria was a narcissistic disorder and stood in a certain relation to paranoia, equivalent to the relationship of conversion hysteria to anxiety hysteria.

This was fundamentally Mrs Klein's position on persecutory or paranoid anxieties until the 1946 paper on splitting mechanisms and projective identification which added a whole new dimension of complexity to the investigation. Although her early theories included splitting of the object into good and bad, it did not include a parallel splitting of the self into good and bad. The bad objects were somehow feared, but if you follow the clinical description, the persecutory anxieties that she describes in the children mainly come from damaged good objects rather than from bad objects. Of the objects that have been split in this splitting-and-idealization, it is the attacks on the good objects which result in persecution while the bad objects mainly produce frustration and deprivation. It was in this way that she discovered phenomena related to the early stages of the Oedipus complex corresponding to Freud's description of the harshness and primitiveness of the superego which he attributed to the distribution of death instinct.

'Notes on some schizoid mechanisms', with its description of splitting mechanisms and projective identification, brought a new complexity to the field. For these splitting mechanisms dismembered the unity of the self as a structure, opening up the prospect of intra-systemic conflict. If the self could be divided, either by splitting-and-idealization, or on other planes of cleavage, the segments could be in conflict with one another. For instance, persecution could come from directions other than retaliation from objects that have been damaged by the child's sadistic attack. That is, the persecution of the idealized part of the self by bad parts of the self could be recognized and this gradually developed into later insights about narcissistic organization. But it also brought about the possibility of seeing the operation of projective identification, for instance, in a fusion of the bad part of the self with the bad objects, producing a quite malignant 'self-object', as Michael Fordham has called them.

What is still muddled in the clinical work of 1941 is clarified in the notes this week, which were written in the late fifties, when a further advance was made, as Mrs Klein began to recognize something more about confusion between good and bad. This is related to two possibilities. This area of confusion was described in *Envy and Gratitude* as attributable to an inadequate splitting-and-idealization, which does not sufficiently separate the idealized from the bad object or the idealized part of the self from the bad part of the self. But confusion can also be brought about by bad parts of the self intruding into good objects. The first of these, that is the inadequate splitting-and idealization, is reflected a bit in Richard's material. In order to function as a prelude to normal development, splitting-and idealization must apparently create mirror images, that is, objects that are complete in themselves but mirror images of one another, one being the idealized and the other the bad one, distinguishable not in their form but only in their qualities and performances.

When splitting-and-idealization functions along other planes of cleavages, for instance where an attempt is made to make the bottom half good and the top half bad or the front good and the back bad, or the breast good and the nipple bad, great difficulties are generated because of the tendency of these splittings-and-idealizations to collapse or for confusion to arise when attempts at integrating the good and bad are brought to bear. This is clear in Richard's case, that splitting and idealization has been attempted along sexual lines, causing the Oedipus complex to be fraught with confusion. The frightening intercourse seems to be a consequence of Richard having attempted to keep the daddy or the penis bad and the mummy or the breast good, so that every time any conjunction of the masculine and feminine object occurred, it produced a confluence of goodness and badness, generating confusion in Richard's mind.

But the other thing that this week reveals is the paranoid anxieties – and demonstrates how different they are from persecutory anxieties. The paranoid object, represented by Cook and Bessie, arises from projective identification, where the split-off bad part of the self penetrates into the good object. It then seems to be good but is in fact malignant and vicious. This is the paranoid object – the breasts that secretly speak German, while on the surface they look like a nice English cook and maid. Unfortunately, we do not have two words for distinguishing between being confused and feeling confused, like we have 'hopelessness' and 'despair'. They are two words which seem to be very much alike but become useful once they are used to express the difference between a hopelessness that is still grasping after hope and is very painful and a despair that has given up hope and is no longer in pain. But we do not have a good way of distinguishing between confusion that is fraught with uncertainty and confusion that is solidified in an object that looks good but is bad, as when there is a beautiful appearance but malignant intentions. The paranoid object is of this quality.

This approach therefore takes 'persecutory anxiety' as a general term under which 'paranoid anxiety' would be subsumed.

We can therefore describe at least six different kinds of persecutory anxieties. First, one can be persecuted internally or in an externalized, projected form by a bad part of the self that can tyrannize, corrupt, frighten, seduce, threaten, propagandize to magnify jealousy and distrust, and in these ways to attack the relationship to the good object. Secondly, one can be persecuted by bad objects which seem primarily bent on tyrannical control, frustration, enslavement, the equivalent of Freud's superego – not the kind of daddy Schreber had, who really seems to have been sadistic to children – but the good puritanical mummy and daddy who think 'spare the rod and spoil the child'.

There is the third type of persecution that comes from damage done to good objects by sadistic attacks upon them. Mrs Klein saw this as mainly related to masturbation attacks of various sorts. This persecution by good objects seems fairly clearly what is now called 'persecutory depression'; that it, when recognizing the damage one has done to good objects, one feels persecuted by these damaged objects because of being unable to bear the depressive feeling, despairing of reparation.

Fourth, there is the severe persecutory anxiety that comes from the formation of a rather malignant bad object through projective identification and fusion between the bad part of the self and the bad object. It produces the bad uncle figure, the bad big brother who is confused with the big daddy. This is the tyrant, the really sadistic tyrant, as distinct from the puritanical and harsh parent or super-ego. Perhaps it is Bion's 'super'-ego.

Fifth is the paranoid object that seems to be due to projective identification of a malignant part of the self into the good objects, especially the breast. This is closely related to Richard's material, of phases of the moon filled in with black, the circle on the paper with the pencil almost shoved through it, Cook and Bessie speaking German, the poison in the bottles. It is also related to his distrust of himself and the bottle that he gives his mother, distrust of his own capacity for love, his secrecy, his tendency to conspiracy.

Finally, sixth, there is a special terror of dead objects, becoming apparent in the material about the sinking of the Hood, the uncertainty if dead people can come back to life and about ghosts. It is also important to remember that when confusion is added to persecution, there comes a tremendous tendency to act out, that is, to test in action what cannot be rationalized in thought.

Sixth week: sessions 30–33

The development of the concept of reparation: true, manic and mock reparation

These four sessions bring into focus an important aspect of the development of Mrs Klein's work, the concept of reparation. It has a very confusing beginning and winds gently through her work, never really drawn together anywhere, in spite of the book she wrote with Joan Riviere in 1937: *Love, Hate and Reparation.*

Again in this week, we meet a contaminated field, because Richard missed the first three sessions, and after his unusual extra session on Sunday became ill again. In a way the week is split into two, the first two sessions being devoted to his recovery from the terrific paranoid and hypochondriacal reactions to his illness and those sessions of the previous week which probably precipitated it, and then the last two sessions devoted mainly to the excitement of having an extraordinary session that arouses both his jealousy and his curiosity. The outbreak of paranoia is particularly linked to his having a sore throat and becomes connected with his hostility towards his father and Paul and the wish for the hook to stick in their throats, like the salmon which might die because of the hook.

The transference context of that material is devoted to mistrust of Mrs Klein, his hostility to her, not just to the 'brute'

Mrs Klein. He wants to swear, using the word 'bloody' to assault her. She seems very relieved when he specifically indicates his wish to assault her. She is probably a bit wrong in the beginning of the first session when she takes up the 'Melanie' as a feeling of having a good mummy inside him. Quite likely it is a bit of cheekiness and patronization, treating her as a servant, like Cook and Bessie. She corrects herself quickly enough to pick up his paranoia. She is able to link it back to that confession of his fear of being poisoned by Cook and Bessie and she says quite promptly that he is feeling poisoned by her the moment he has pain in his tummy, feeling that she is really feeding him a fish hook.

He recovers quite nicely, which she tends to attribute almost entirely to her interpretations, but something important has changed in her demeanour towards Richard in response to his asking her for help. He asks repeatedly that she put out the lights, fill in his drawings for him, and finally says 'Do something for me', and Mrs Klein realizes that he does not know what it is he wants her to do. He is acknowledging his helplessness and his dependence upon her, after having previously told her rather courageously, that he thought 'the work' would do no good. However, in the second session, he tells her that it is doing him good, and later on in the week there is more feeling in it. He needs her help but does not know what he needs, except that it has something to do with his feeling so frightened of other children and that his fear somehow provokes other children to violence towards him. When later in the week he tells her that he has gathered a little more courage, it is immediately consecrated to do terrible things to all his enemies after the war. But being able to think about after the war also means that he has recovered some hopefulness, not only about his internal war, but of the external war as well. It contrasts with his mood when he told his mother that he would commit suicide if the Germans invaded.

There is a very marked change in his hopefulness and his trust in Mrs Klein, along with an increased interest in her work. This change seems due, not to the interpretations which were not very different from previous ones, nor is the material much differ-ent, but largely to his asking her for help and her responding in a way that seems to mark a change in her feeling for him.

These eruptions of his hate, of violence and cruelty, of terror and paranoia have generated a more serious conception of the severity of his illness and the nature of his constitutional problems. Mrs Klein seems now much more impressed that he has a really difficult temperament to cope with and that there is something very brutally sadistic and cold in him, augmented by possessive jealousy. Its eruption absolutely sweeps him along and there seems to be nothing he can do about it. This change in Mrs Klein produces a marked increase in Richard's trust and hopefulness about the treatment. However, this beneficial shift is interfered with by his excitement about seeing her on Sunday. Why does she not always see him on Sunday? Who does she see on Sunday? Her son and grandson? His usual intrusive jealousy tries to ferret out this information. All in all, it is a very satisfactory week and mobilizes his constructive and reparative tendencies.

In *The Psychoanalysis of Children*, and the early papers, such as the one on criminality, Mrs Klein used the term 'restitution' not 'reparation'. Generally this stemmed from her studies of the pregenital period and particularly those aspects she later called the paranoid-schizoid position. She was greatly impressed by the greed and stealing; the child robbing the mother of her faeces, her internal penises, babies, and other phantasied riches. If the child could tolerate guilt and was not so persecuted by dead or damaged objects, it could begin to try to restore some good relationship. This often resulted in the child attempting to give back what it had stolen, to make restitution. In *The Psychoanalysis of Children* she speaks much more cogently of the omnipotence with which this is carried out; not only the attacks but the restitution as well, are carried out by omnipotent means. But the importance of this issue tended to be lost for a number of years. This is reflected at many points in her interpretative work with Richard. Her mode of presentation seems to lay stress on his active attempts at restitution, later called 'restoration' and finally 'reparation'. Her recognition of the omnipotence by which these active measures are carried out by the child seems to get lost until *Envy and Gratitude* (1957), although there is some mention of it in the 1946 paper on schizoid mechanisms.

The difference between true reparation and various forms of manic activity (later called 'manic reparation' and 'mock reparation') carried out by omnipotence, does not really become clear before the very end of Mrs Klein's work. Some notes in this book are her most succinct and advanced statements on the subject. The shift from calling it restitution to calling it restoration and finally reparation is not simply a shift based on recognitition of the role of omnipotence. The greater complexity of the child, attacks on the mother's body, both its motives and its means, were defined first in 'Notes on some schizoid mechanisms' and later in *Envy and Gratitude*. For instance, the jealousy of the internal babies arose on two scores: first of all jealousy of their imagined blissful existence inside the mother and secondly the jealousy of them as potential new babies that would be born to take possession of the breasts. Also, there developed a greater complexity in her thinking about the nature of the attacks. Smashing to pieces calls for different means of reparation from stealing. She interprets to Richard that he feels he wants to put together all the pieces but feels incapable of doing so. Richard clearly reacts with feelings of being overwhelmed by the task that she seems to be presenting to him. She seems to require that he perform such onerous tasks as putting together all the smashed and broken objects, giving the mother more babies with his good penis, as well as fighting and defeating this Hitler part of himself. Her response to his plaintive breakdown, asking for help, later accompanied by his touching her neck, which she recognizes means touching her breasts, links back to the little paper on art, about the operetta of Ravel with the libretto written by Colette. Instancing the libretto, Mrs Klein refers to her concept of reparation as an illustration, describing the child as having a temper tantrum of smashing. He becomes persecuted by all the broken furniture which had come to life to threaten him. But finally a squirrel that is dying moves him to pity and he tries to bandage it. At that moment all the persecution disappears, the animals and the furniture that had come to life are very sympathetic to him and say he is a good boy. At that time he calls for help, saying 'Mamma'. Somehow the importance of his saying 'Mamma' tends to be a little bit lost in the admiration that Mrs Klein, as well as the animals, feel for the bandaging, so that the fact of his feeling utterly helpless to repair all the damage, and being able to call for help is perhaps undervalued. It became a bit lost in her general theory about reparation.

To begin with then, reparation was seen as a very active process with the mental significance of reversing all the damage. But Mrs Klein recognized that, when children attempt to put into action their reparative impulses, they experience a terrible incapacity and frustration. They discover that it is terribly easy to break things and terribly hard to put them together. Her ideas about reparation were set in flux. As a purely internal process the child can in his phantasy and feelings omnipotently repair all the damage that is done, but only at the expense of being caught on the manic treadmill, *Sorcerer's Apprentice* fashion.

It is important to note that around this time when she was developing a concept of reparation, Mrs Klein used the concept of sublimation in a very integrated way in her theories, but very differently from the way Freud had used it. She puts forward the idea that the drive to reparation is the main stimulus to sublimation and therefore sublimations are in fact reparative acts. She cites the woman doing the painting, suddenly and impulsively, having been in a state of mental anguish because somebody had taken a painting off her wall and the empty space was tormenting her with depression. She painted a picture herself of a naked negress, demonstrating an extraordinary talent, although she had never painted before. It was entirely different from Freud's idea that sublimation was a rather tricky way of directing one's polymorphously perverse infantile sexual impulses into action in the outside world in a socially acceptable and desexualized way.

She also distinguished at this time between 'reactive tendencies' in a manner again very different from Freud's use of 'reaction formation'. He conceived a manipulation of affects to alter the direction of impulse into its opposite. Mrs Klein used 'reactive tendencies' to describe forms of activity which are intended either to prevent the damage of assault on the objects or to reverse the damage in some way particularly connected with reparation. This seems to be her position with reference to reparation until the 1946 paper on schizoid mechanisms.

First of all she began to differentiate the motivation: between manic reparation as defence against persecutory or depressive anxiety; and something much more genuinely in the service of the objects. Secondly, as a result of the discovery of split-ting processes and projective identification, her conception of the mechanics of reparation moved to a deeper level. Whereas previously her descriptions of unconscious phantasy had a very concrete quality to them, there was less emphasis on the meaning of the child's masturbatory phantasies of assaults on his objects. At the height of his sadistic period in the oral and anal phases he chopped them to pieces and burnt them, etc. The recognition of splitting processes and projective identification implied the understanding that these assaults were not simply raw impulse run wild, nor simple revenges or robbing, but that they have a meaning in psychic reality related to the structure of the person-ality. From this point of view, the meaning of these assaults was seen as twofold. One is a splitting type of assault and the other is a projective type of assault. That is, one type of assault creates a split in the object; something that was a single object before is now two objects. So splitting attacks result in a multiplication of objects. The other kind of assault by projection has the meaning of taking something from the self and putting it into the object. This brings about the psychological state in which your own self seems now to be lacking in something and the object to have something added to it.

From this viewpoint reparations can also have a structural meaning, not merely the concrete sense of putting broken bits together again or giving back the goodies. How was the struc tural alteration and its meaning for self and object to be undone or reversed? What could the self do and what would have to be done by the objects? And what would be the mental economics of such recovery? Such questions began to produce the realization that the child could not put the bits together, he could not give mummy new babies, he could not heal the splits. Perhaps he could take back a projective identification as the active compo-nent that the self can perform in reparation.

But on the whole, reparation began to take on a more mysteri-ous meaning, something that happens in the depressive position. That frame of mind of depressive feeling, guilt or remorse or just regret, or wishing it had not happened, seems to make possible the process by which objects repair one another. The distinc-tion between the active and passive components immediately galvanizes the understanding of the difference between manic reparation and true reparation. The true reparation is something that happens when the mental condition, the mental atmosphere is conducive to the objects repairing one another.

This gave an entirely new meaning to the concept of the primal scene; not simply mummy and daddy enjoying one another or making babies. A specific function of repairing the splitting infused a new urgency to the parental coition: mummy must repair daddy's penis and daddy's penis must repair mummy's breasts and thus reconstitute the combined object. These two components, a part which the self can perform by taking back its projective identifications through accepting its depressive feeling, and a part which the objects can do for one another in their coition when infantile dependence is acknowledged, restore the damage that has been produced primarily by masturbation attacks. Mrs Klein's work with Richard marks a turning point in her views on reparation. The sessions this week bring a change in her orientation to him. She is much more helpful and nurturing to him in his greater acknowledgement of helplessness. Her helpfulness is largely centered on the interpretive process, but also emerges in little services at his request.

CHAPTER SEVEN

Seventh week: sessions 34–39

Concepts of confusion – their absence in the work with Richard and its consequence

An interesting week, but again it is a week that is interfered with because, on the Tuesday, Mrs Klein tells Richard that her trip to London is to start at the end of the week. He does not really react to this information until Thursday, and then on Friday and Saturday it strikes him terribly. So it is another one of those weeks in which the setting has been interfered with – the mother's illness, Mrs Klein going away, the playroom being locked so that she has to take him to her lodgings. There is hardly a week that has not been interfered with in some way, but it is very instructive to see how the interferences and the analytic process somehow mingle with one another.

By this time in the analysis almost all Richard's insincerity has dropped away, at least temporarily, and this is a week in which there is very little resistance to the analytical work. His participation has become somehow less formalized; although he plays with the fleet and draws a few Empire drawings, the really important things that happen just erupt – suddenly he digs in Mrs Klein's bag; he rushes out of the room into the kitchen and squirts the water; emotionality pours from him, looking up at her eyes, saying how he loves her. This analysis is going at full pace, and

Richard is passionately involved in it, already feeling that it has benefited him. He tells her so, and his mother confirms this, that some of his fear of school children has diminished. He is beginning to be able to think of himself as possibly grown up someday.

With all this the attachment to the analysis and to Mrs Klein in the transference is becoming very manifest. It is true that she continues her mode of interpreting, rather unlike her general technique, continually referring to Mummy and Daddy and Paul. When she does that quite a lot she meets strong obstacles in him, indicating that he would much rather deal with the transference, about Mrs Klein and Mr Klein and her son and grandson, about what is happening in the war, to act it out there in the playroom, and not have it pushed back into his home situation where things are much less clear to him.

Our main approach has been to study Mrs Klein's work historically and to follow the development of her technique and theoretical equipment but it is also instructive to notice the theoretical equipment she was not yet working with and the ways in which it left her in the lurch. That is probably the way psychoanalysis develops, that an analyst has the feeling of being left in the lurch by his framework of understanding, and begins to search for some other way. The formulations he is using just are not containing the situation and helping it develop. In 1941 Mrs Klein did not as yet have a workable concept of confusion, as a close examination of part of a session will show. Even when confusion is not central, Richard's material can be difficult to follow because various threads of material move rather simultaneously and interweave. It is incredibly interesting and one can imagine how challenging it must have been to work with this child who kept shifting his modes of representation – one minute rushing out of the room onto the steps, the next minute the fleet play, then telling her dreams or bits of information, and then back again to the fleet play. It is questionable how to understand this continual shift of mode of representation. The shifting comes about in a way that tempts one to say, as with earlier sessions, 'play disruption'. But now one is impressed that the shift in the nature of the material has much more the significance of changed mode of communication. It is as if Richard said, 'No, you don't get it yet. Suppose I jump down the steps; now do you get it?'

This continual shifting of representation, although it is taxing for Mrs Klein, also allows her, just as continually, to rectify her interpretation and reach better approximations in her understanding.

By this week it is very clear to her that Richard is constantly asking her for help, mainly by his attitude but sometimes in concrete requests such as the time he puts the stools on one another, knocks them over and asks her to help him build them up again. The interpretations also veer towards emphasis on his helplessness in the fact of the violence of the impulses which produce the catastrophes. She is more pointedly investigating his masturbation and even presses him to acknowledgement, which is rather relieving to him. She has a particular way of talking about masturbation simply as a fact and relating it a bit to the kind of material that will illustrate for him the sort of unconscious phantasies that accompany his masturbation. She does not seem to link the masturbation to the functions and phantasies about his penis, which emerge in the concreteness of the material. She does not, for example, interpret to him that his penis is his hand digging into her bag, or that his penis is like his hand digging into the dirt, or his father's penis is like the crane that handed the jack-in-the-box to him. Instead of making the masturbation phantasy very vivid to him by linking it strongly with the material, she seems to be introducing him very gently to the idea that these are phantasies that accompany masturbation, implying that it is not the masturbation itself, but the meaning of the masturbation that is important.

Regarding the development of the material of the week, the very striking thing is the intensity of relationship with the breasts that is beginning to show through. It comes out particularly on the Thursday and Friday, somewhat under the pressure of her imminent holiday, but the impression created is that although the breast material may be increased in intensity by the imminence of the holiday, it has not been propelled out of sequence, as was, for example, the intense depressive feeling forced forward by his mother's illness in the third week. Mrs Klein going to London and the threat to her of being bombed or the possibility of his having to go to her funeral are all very vivid to Richard and stir concern for her but mainly for himself in his need for analysis. He handles it in a manful way, asking, should she die, who could continue his analysis. Clearly he feels that there is something quite unique going on in his relationship with Mrs Klein that will not easily be replaceable. He makes her promise to go to the air raid shelter and to give his mother the name of another analyst. This is very impressive. For a young boy, in the midst of feeling attached to Mrs Klein and leaning his head against her, to whom she looks beautiful like the hills outside, to be able to grasp that it is the analysis he needs and that in this respect she is potentially replaceable, shows surprising discrimination.

Of course Richard does not take it all in for the first two days but continues in an obviously manic way with the fleet play in which somehow peace is to be kept in the family. But this time is not the peace of everybody having equal shares, as in the empire drawings and in the fleet play where no one was to touch the mummy ship or was to have any special intimate relation. In this material, particularly in the harbour gate episode, and Richard laughing about the pigs trying to get into the pigsty and his account about the chickens – how the cock had his head in the hen house and how their bellies shook – the emphasis has shifted from everybody having equal shares to one-at-a-time. The good stuff is down there in the harbour/ genitals and all the men – Mr Klein, he, Paul, Daddy – get their turn and get what they need, which is not necessarily the same as what they want or equal. So there has been a considerable advance in his concept of justice – the progress from egalitarianism to each-according-to-his-need. The mummy is a rich mummy, the rich machine from which he got the jack-in-the box, the woman who gave him the liquorice.

In this context, Richard's second experience in Mrs Klein's lodgings is not very exciting. He is much more in awe, frightened that the 'grumpy old man' would be about and a bit worried that this was not the right place for his analysis. He does not really like that session very much and is very relieved to get back to the play room the next day. This seems a good indication of progress with his greediness. This piggy greediness that was mainly attached to his penis is coming up into his mouth and being directed to the breasts. It is at this point that he becomes very confused and Mrs Klein does not have the conceptual equipment to help him. The problem of confusion which he represents variously by the jumping down the steps, by going in and out of the house to watch the water drain away seems to involve various dimensions of relation to the maternal object – inside/outside, upstairs/downstairs, frontside/backside, and all in the matrix of uncertainty about the good and the bad in his object.

To illustrate how the lack of a piece of conceptual equipment could interfere with her grasping things about the material, we must examine the session itself. This is from the Thursday session (towards the bottom of page 177):

> Richard had become restless, he walked over to the map and studied how much there was of occupied and unoccupied France. He again wondered how the allies were getting on with Syria. Then he went outside and, as usual, called Mrs Klein to come too. He looked round and said he did not like seeing the sky overcast. He repeatedly jumped down from the steps, which were fairly high, and said it was fun. He said he was looking forward to playing croquet with the Polish soldiers.
>
> Mrs Klein interpreted that the soldiers stood for the nice Daddy who would help him become potent, would teach him (croquet) and treat him like an equal, which also meant that he would also help him to be equal in sexual matters – to have sexual intercourse with Mummy and give her children. [*That is the theme she is on, of his wanting to be potent and his concern about his penis and masturbation. She has not picked up the greediness of the penis and its function of getting in like a hand in her bag, that is, its prehensile capability. She is thinking more of his desire to use his penis to give babies to Mummy, to thank her, repay her, protect her.*] His pleasure in jumping well had the same significance.
>
> Richard kept on running up and down the footpath. Suddenly he asked Mrs Klein to go quickly back into the room with him; he had seen a wasp. [*He was not really very frightened of the wasp, but was dramatizing.*]
>
> Mrs Klein followed him into the room and interpreted that the footpath represented her inside and genital, running up and down and jumping from the steps meant sexual intercourse with her; the dangerous wasp stood for the hostile Daddy and Paul inside Mummy, or Mrs Klein's son or Mr Klein inside Mrs Klein.

Richard played with the stools and piled some of them on top of each other. He pointed out to Mrs Klein that he had again made a big tower [*as he had on the Monday session when it had fallen down and he had asked her to help him put it up again*] and the way in which he said it plainly showed that he was thinking of the tower which had to be dynamited [*his reference to the Crystal Palace tower, 34th session.*] He knocked the stools down and said, 'Poor Daddy, here is his genital tumbling down.' [*He tried to go along with her interpretation quite sincerely. But there is some considerable difference between falling down and getting hurt, and jumping down quite skilfully.*] Then he remarked on a man passing by on the road, said he was nasty and might do him some harm. He watched the man, hiding behind the curtain until he disappeared from sight. [*That seems a bit of genuine anxiety connected with his trying to go along with her interpretation of dynamiting Daddy's penis, and in consequence, becoming persecuted by the daddy again.*]

Mrs Klein interpreted that though he was sorry for Daddy if he attacked Daddy's genital, he also felt that Daddy would turn into an attacker and injure Richard's genital (mixture of depressive and persecutory anxiety). That was why he was suddenly frightened of the 'nasty' man (the wasp) and had been so afraid of children in previous sessions. The boys not only stood for Daddy and Paul and the attacked babies, but also Daddy's attacked genital.

Richard had gone back to the table and looked at the drawing, reminding Mrs Klein to date it. He said he would like to see all the drawings next day. Then he pointed at the blue section which had no coastline because he had divided it off by a pencil line and asked Mrs Klein whether she knew what this represented. But he answered the question at once himself: 'It was Mummy's breast.' [*This is how he goes to another representation as if to say 'Wait a second, you didn't get it; now I'm talking about jumping down from Mummy's breasts to Mummy's genitals and how, when I do that, the wasp comes. But up at Mummy's breasts it is much better'.*] He mentioned for the second time that a lady at the hotel had given him liquorice – she was very nice. He now looked happy and very friendly, and putting his arm very lightly round Mrs Klein's shoulder and leaning his head against her, he said 'I'm very fond of you.'

Mrs Klein interpreted the connection between her, as helpful and protective, and Mummy's feeding breast – the lady's liquorice. Also, by co-operating with Mrs Klein and asking her to preserve the drawings he wished to return to Mrs Klein what she had given him. [*One can see how she allows herself to be corrected.*] Richard particularly felt that she was good to him, and fed him with her good breast because the work she was doing with him had made him less frightened about his genital. Richard replied that he thought so too. He ran into the kitchen, turned on the tap and made the water squirt by putting his finger inside the tap and listened to the noise it made. [*It was very impulsive, she mentioned the word genitals and he's off.*] He said that this was Daddy's genital and that it sounded very angry. Then by putting his finger into the tap in a different way he made the water squirt differently and said that this was himself – he too was angry. [*One cannot escape the impression that he is angry with her for having mentioned genitals, about her making him frightened of them, when it is quite clear that he is feeling that to be the baby at the breast has made him less hostile to everybody and therefore less persecuted by other children, wasps, and grumpy old men. But it is not his genitals being preserved that has brought relief. His general persecutory anxiety has been relieved because there has been some diminution in his own general feeling of hostility to everybody.*]

Mrs Klein interpreted that he had shown that his own and his father's genitals were fighting inside her (the tap); he expected Daddy or Mr Klein to be angry with him if he put his genital inside Mummy or Mrs Klein.

Richard went outside and asked Mrs Klein to pull the plug out of the sink so that he 'could see the water running away'. Then he found a bit of coal and crushed it with his foot. [*In the last session he had crushed the female doll with his foot in reaction to Mrs Klein going away. He had put his Hitler boot on it, but carefully, under the instep, so that in effect he did not crush it. Now he does actually crush the piece of coal.*]

Mrs Klein interpreted that he was destroying his father's black genital. [*By bringing him back to the genitals, and in that way reminding him of the father's genitals, she has functioned as a breast which flaunts the nipple and reminds the infant of the father's penis and of the mother's intercourse with him. This is seen as black and bad and arouses a pregenital oedipal attack on the breast and nipple as a combined object.*] Richard fetched the broom, swept the floor and said he would like to clean up the whole place.

Mrs Klein suggested that if he felt he destroyed Daddy's genital inside Mummy, he would also dirty and injure her, and then would wish to put her right again. [*The point is that when he found the bit of coal and crushed it he was outside and now he wants to clean up the room inside. Probably inside the room has the same relation to outside at this time as the top of the steps has to the bottom of the steps – up at the breasts and down at the genitals. Richard seems to be saying again here that it is the daddy-penis outside that he attacks but if inside or up at the breasts he feels very helpful and would, as it were, like to lick the breast and make it lovely and clean.*] Richard went back to playing with the tap. He said he was thirsty and drank from the tap. Then he asked Mrs Klein if she knew what he had been drinking, and again without waiting for a reply, he said, 'Little Job' [*that is, urine. He shows extremely clearly at this point that he is struggling with some confusion between nipple and penis, and whether this tap is a nipple which gives milk from the breasts or is it daddy's penis which is presiding over, or possessing, the breasts and urinating into his mouth*].

This material gives the impression of Mrs Klein being inadequately equipped to understand what Richard is struggling very hard to tell her, that something is going on in his relationship with the breasts. He distrusts the feeling that he has when his arm is lightly around her and he says he's fond of her because the moment she mentions genitals he becomes confused, as if instead of milk, urine had come into the baby's mouth.

Seeing such difficult material tackled with inadequate conceptual equipment helps one to understand a little bit the historical perspective in psychoanalysis. It is not like saying 'What did they do before TV?', but more like wondering how people ever tolerated loving children when they knew that more than half of them were going to die in childhood. Mrs Klein at that point in

1940/41 was struggling to understand something about a child's approach to the breasts and the way it was being interfered with by Richard's anxieties about her going to London and the fear of her being killed. At the same time, her going off to London means to him that she is going to see her son and grandson and that it is indistinguishable from her going on holiday. This in turn means the same as going to see Mr Klein and having intercourse with him, although Richard knows Mr Klein is dead. It confronts him with this Oedipus complex at a pregenital level, which Mrs Klein knows a lot about. But what she does not know much about at this point is how it is that the genital Oedipus complex impinges itself on a baby's relationship with the breasts. She does not know anything about these kinds of confusion, that the two breasts can be making love to one another, the two nipples can be homosexuals sucking on one another, etc. Consequently she has to struggle with this sort of material while still fairly inadequately equipped. But by the fifteenth week you will see that she has worked it all out with Richard's help. Both he and Mrs Klein seem suddenly to realize that four months of analysis is not very much. He has already had almost two months with her and there are only two months more. He is getting the wind up about it and she is realizing also how much needs to be done for this boy and how little she is going to accomplish. Mrs Klein writes a sad little note about what the mother told her – how much better Richard is. While it is true, both he and she were feeling pretty desperate about having only a few months more. Perhaps it helps one to understand this other aspect of her technique in this case which seems to be different from that which she usually followed, that is, referring back to the family situation instead of drawing it all into the transference. Mrs Klein may quite reasonably have been afraid of involving him in the depth and intensity of transference that would make the ending not only terribly painful but possibly insupportable to him.

CHAPTER EIGHT

Eighth week: sessions 40–45

*The phenomenology of hypochondria: its differentiation
from psychosomatic phenomena or somatic delusions*

T his is the week following Mrs Klein's return from her
nine days in London. It starts on the Tuesday and goes
through to include Sunday and is a week that is very
sharply divided. In the first session Richard is very persecuted
about coming back to X and persecuted also by Mrs Klein.
He does not really regain his relationship to her until the next
session when he confesses his infidelity or, really, betrayal of
her during the break. He had apparently seduced his mother by
telling her she was a better analyst than Mrs Klein because she
was his mother. Once Mrs Klein has related this to the breast-
transference, contact is restored.

In the week before Mrs Klein went away she seemed to be
emphasizing castration anxiety and only sporadically recognizing the infantile transference to the breast and the horizontal
splitting of the mother into the breast-mummy upstairs and a
very sexual and potentially bad and seductive mummy down
stairs. This is the material that presents itself immediately in the
Tuesday session, where he seems to have externalized that split on
to his good mother at home and Mrs Klein as the bad mummy,
surrounded or filled with poisonous nettles and toadstool babies.

65

Again he stamps on his rivals and again the phantasy of being poisoned comes out when he gets his sore throat. That theme of the splitting of the mother into the idealized light blue breast-mummy who gives him his shredded wheat and this bad old woman genital spitting yellow stuff now also invades the Empire drawings so that it looks like a horrid bird which has black stuff falling out of it. (This is the material Mrs Klein used for her 1945 paper 'The Oedipus complex in the light of early anxiet-ies'.) When he cannot keep the split going, Richard either gets a sore throat or feels that he has poison dripping down inside him. It is instructive to note how different is this confusional and persecuted state from the paranoid delusion of being poisoned by the secret German spies, Cook and Bessie.

The manic material which follows the confession of seducing his mother seems to have two determinants. One of these he confessed to on the Saturday – that he was sleeping in the same room as his mother because of limited hotel accommodation. It was also determined by Mrs Klein letting him off much too easily, by not making it quite clear to him that during the separa-tion there had been an element of betrayal, leaving her to be bombed and killed in London. Her excessive gentleness often has the consequence of Richard becoming rather manic, feeling that 'Larry the Lamb' has triumphed over truth.

The next few sessions are very much influenced by feeling that now Mrs Klein has become the good, light-blue as well as his mummy, whom he has both day and night. He and Mummy are the king and queen and his Daddy and Paul are reduced to babies, little piggies trying to get into the pigsty. The manic triumph is also represented by the long red thing going all the way through the empire drawing (No. 27), which Mrs Klein astutely ties up with his lining up his ships and seeing they are straight. She inter-prets a manic acquisition of all the rival genitals and appending them to his own penis. In a way the mania does not so much break down as a result of Mrs Klein's interpretations; somehow it just seems to collapse very suddenly as bits of persecution appear. There are two men talking outside and he is spying on them and they are spying on him; a horrid old woman is spitting this nasty yellow stuff, and then he comes back the next day with a sore throat and persecuted. There is no doubt in his mind that it is tied up with this semi-delusion that Cook and Bessie are poisoning him. When Mrs Klein recognized the implication that she and the mother had become the two idealized breasts which now suddenly turned into these very bad and poisonous buttocks (the horrid bird), she is able to afford him very great relief.

The next day, of course, he is filled with gratitude and admiration for her in her silver dress and her lovely hair. The idealization builds up again, represented by the shredded wheat that he has had from his mother, which allayed his gnawing hunger and protruding bones. It was from material like this that Mrs Klein built up her concept of persecutory and depressive hypochondria as the mainstay phenomena for the concept of the concreteness of psychic reality.

Freud, when he wrote the paper 'On narcissism', cited hypochondria as one of the general evidences for narcissism as a stage between autoerotism and object relations. In hypochondria, the libido regressed to narcissistic libido, was concentrated on the body and this produced the hypochondriacal symptoms, which Freud took mainly as obsessional.

In *The Psychoanalysis of Children*, Mrs Klein noted hypochondriacal symptoms as one of the very common complaints of children. In the 1920s and early 1930s, her ideas were still very attached to the libido theory, but had been modified now by her concepts of projection and introjection as continual processes. Her view of hypochondria was in a way similar to Freud's: but where Freud expressed the dynamic in terms of withdrawal of the libido from objects onto the ego, she tended to express it as withdrawal of the libido from external objects onto internal objects. In a certain way, this seemed to imply that she was talking about narcissistic phenomena in Freud's sense of narcissistic libido. This first attempt to formulate hypochondriacal phenomena in terms of libido theory and the interaction of projection and introjection only qualified as narcissism because it involved the cutting off of the person's interest in the outside world, corresponding to Freud's idea of withdrawal of object libido.

By 1934, in the paper on manic-depressive states, when she was already further along in considering the interplay between paranoid-schizoid and depressive phenomena she was in a position to recognize and describe two different types of hypochondria.

She first delineated hypochondria of the type she had talked of in *The Psychoanalysis of Children*, in which the person feels attacked internally, attacked in the self by bad objects, but she also described a depressive kind of hypochondria in which the good objects are being attacked, internally, by the bad objects and the id. If she had gone back to it later after the paper on schizoid-mechanisms she probably would have described the two types of hypochondria differently, one that was dominated by depressive concern for the objects represented by the organ that was afflicted, the other dominated by persecutory guilt, in which the person wanted to get rid of the afflicted organ. This takes hypochondria as a single phenomenon, in which parts of the body are seen to be identified with internal objects that are suffering in some way, and one may either have a depressive relationship to the suffering or a persecutory one. She would not have had the means of distinguishing between hypochondria and somatic delusion or psychosomatic phenomena. The phenomena Richard reports this week seem to be a mixture of all three, a sore throat as a depressive psychosomatic phenomenon, a somatic delusion of internal poisoning and persecutory hypochondria about his gnawing hunger and protruding bones. The mechanisms that produce hypochondria were becoming apparent to Mrs Klein at the time she treated Richard, but she did not have the equipment to elucidate it. Note I (p. 216) goes some distance in doing that, since she recognized that it had something to do with identification processes, that it was linked to Freud's and Abraham's conception of melancholia. She saw that hypochondria stood very close to melancholia through identification with damaged objects and that the struggle had to do with the way the identification processes altered emotionality, so that instead of feelings of guilt on the one hand or persecution on the other, the person tended to feel self-pity, projected as clamorous demands for reparation of the self, or to be rid of the damaged object by surgical means. The only very significant addendum to that conception of hypochondria that one could add from more recent works is most plainly described by Dr Rosenfeld. The hypochondriac, like the melancholic, is in a rather double bond of identifications; he is not only projectively identified with the internal object that is damaged (and partly it is damaged as a result of the projective identification) but is also identified with this object introjectively. Thus he is caught in a rather double system of identification from which it is extremely difficult for him to liberate himself.

The other issue that Mrs Klein discusses at some length in her notes on this week (Note 2, p. 216) is the business about integration. The notes about it are really too poorly related to the material to be at all convincing at this point. That whole topic about integration and what she meant by it and how it relates to concepts of splitting are better illustrated in later sessions.

CHAPTER NINE

Ninth week: sessions 46–52

Splitting and idealization – its role in development and its defects' contribution to psychopathology

This week's material springs from the themes of the Monday session, the most important session in the book as regards Richard's disturbances about the shortness of the analysis. This was becoming very real and vivid to him, and to Mrs Klein, for she is again seeing him on Sunday. It is another seven session week. The previous Sunday, which was the sixth session of that week because she had not seen him on the Monday, brought material about her silver dress and lovely hair, and his golden shoes. The atmosphere of the session, which Mrs Klein did not pick up sufficiently, was one of incipient mania which burst on the Monday.

The way in which these Sunday sessions are impinging on him becomes very clear during this week and she finally notes it in the Sunday session itself, when Richard raises the question about her not going to church but seeing him instead. He has a strong suspicion that it is because of greed for money, for he has discovered the facts of her fee, and confronts her with it in rather a devastating way. The other factor in the setting of the week is the expectation of the arrival of his father. Although Richard is looking forward to going fishing with father, the thought of being expelled from his mother's bedroom, which has really been the source of the mania, drives him quite wild. In the Thursday session, the very interesting 'go away Mr Smith, go back to work' material appears, certainly referring forward to his father's coming. All the railway drawings seem under the sway of the expectations of his father's arrival, but are woven into the transference: people crossing, Mr Klein going away sobbing, Richard and Mrs Klein meeting secretly. And there are the various interesting names which she makes use of –'Valing', 'Roseman' and so on. The 'Roseman' quite clearly referred to the hotel manager scolding him for picking the roses. Mrs Klein relates that mainly to his craving for the father's penis, which comes out quite clearly, following on from the earlier material about the 'delicious monster', or the yellow pencil being crammed into every orifice, mouth, ears, nose, in biting the pencil, and in the very interesting phantasy about the mouse in his parents' bedroom. It ate the two biscuits, ran up his father's fishing rod and both father and mother were afraid of it. There is probably a bit of the truth in it, that there was something about the violence in this boy that did intimidate his parents, and made it very difficult for them to maintain any constant curb on his naughtiness, his exhausting his mother, or doing as he pleased.

The collapse of the mania comes on Wednesday with the fascinating Kafkaesque dream about his being tried at a court but not knowing the charge against him. In the Thursday session it transpires that he was charged with breaking a window, and Mrs Klein spots immediately that it is connected with a window being broken in the playroom, although not by Richard. Presumably one of the girl guides had broken it. Nevertheless it is certainly connected intimately with his phantasies because he admits in the Friday or Saturday session that he was very cross in the morning and felt like breaking a window. The idea of breaking a window is closely connected with his Hitler identification, with the bomb that had fallen near his home, smashing the glass house and frightening Cook and Bessie.

The dream reflects the curbing of his manic tyrannical phantasies and helps Mrs Klein to focus on a problem which she says herself was only to be discussed fully some fifteen years later in *Envy and Gratitude*: the problem of splitting-and-idealization.

The notes to the Thursday and Friday session about splitting-and-idealization are some of the most important theoretical-technical notes in the book. Mrs Klein has come to recognize through Richard's material how quickly and easily good objects turn bad for him. He loses his judgment under the slightest stress, and becomes not only persecuted but persecuting. She had already interpreted that if he attacks the father's penis as a persecutor inside the mother, he also attacks and harms the mother. His confusion and difficulty in distinguishing between good and bad in his objects and himself is illustrated by the blackness of his father in the empire drawings which contrasted with his actual love for his father. Now the quickness with which Mr Smith turns bad and then is a quite nice man a few minutes later in the session astonishes Richard.

One might think that this was a problem about which she was very clear for it goes back into her earliest writings, when she talked about the baby splitting the breast into the good and bad breasts. But she did not realize until much later that this critical operation for the establishment of the conditions for growth and development was most difficult and could go wrong in many ways. In this note (III, p. 249) she discusses mainly the two ways it could go wrong quantitatively: inadequate or excessive splitting-and-idealization. In her later work there are hints that she was also aware that it could go wrong in qualitative ways; that is, the plane of splitting could be basically faulty. There is, for instance, the splitting-and-idealization with respect to the mother and father, for one to be idealized and the other to be the bad object. This goes on a bit here – also at part-object level between breast and penis, or between the breast and nipple. A horizontal plane of splitting between the top of the mother's body and the bottom, or between the front and the back, can be attempted, each giving rise to a situation in the child that is unsatisfactory for development.

In this note Mrs Klein explains that it is necessary for the splitting-and-idealization to be sufficiently 'wide' to diminish the persecutory anxiety. That is, the badness must be sufficiently split off so that it is not constantly crowding into and spoiling the secure relationship between the idealized part of the self and the idealized object. On the other hand, it must not be so widely split off as to diminish the anxiety below the level which is necessary for development. This necessary level, probably different in different children, had become apparent to her, mainly by examination of the analytic situation, discovering that patients in analysis needed to maintain a certain level of anxiety in order for the material to come, and for working through to take place.

This problem of inadequate splitting-and-idealization of self and object will henceforth be central in Richard's analysis. He could not keep the destructive and Hitleresque part of himself from crowding in on and taking over the good part. A very clear description of the consequent hypocrisy in his character is brought to light by the Larry-the-Lamb material, how he acts like a lamb while secretly causing all sorts of difficulties. A bit of confusion enters these notes because Mrs Klein has introduced the concept of externalization as well. She felt that the transference was mainly based on externalization of the internal situation. The patient's desire to externalize his internal situation was a way of putting it into the outside world, partly as an evacuation of internal persecution and partly as a way of ridding himself of the complete responsibility for the preservation of his internal objects. She has introduced this concept of externalization into her discussion of splitting-and-idealization in relation to Richard's locating his persecutor in the outside world, as in the 'Now I can kill Hitler' material, when he was holding all these sharpened pencils in his hand, and feeling that he now had the weapons with which to kill his persecutor. That his persecutor could be felt as a real figure in the outside world is an aspect of the externalization and seems to Mrs Klein to be helpful to his development because of the way in which it locates his persecutor and places it at a distance from himself, thus representing a widening of the splitting-and-idealization. She connects it with his being able to be more open himself, which is perhaps not very convincing. The material in the previous week already indicates that Richard was more confiding, more open in his communications, less secretive and less omnipotent in his secrecy. For instance his asking Mrs Klein personal questions about going to church or about her fee, although sprung on her in a slightly tricky way, all represent an improvement in his honesty.

This brings into focus another aspect of her notes, about integration. Although Mrs Klein saw the thirst for knowledge as essentially a thirst for knowledge about the mother's body, representing the child's world and later extended to the world in general, she also saw evidences of a thirst for knowledge about the internal world, psychic reality. She noticed the amount of pleasure that patients could take, and Richard here takes, in discovering things about the unconscious, despite the fact that the discoveries may bring elements of mental pain. She felt this to be the pleasure of integration, of the discovery of little-known parts of oneself, repressed, split off, or not realized in one way or another. This pleasure in the coming together of parts of the self, and feeling more whole, was, in her view, one of the great benefits of the analytical process. In her notes she attributes Richard's pleasure to integration, where he says now he's an American, he feels he's a new man. It may not be a quite correct understanding because he seems a bit manically optimistic at that point, celebrating his transformation. But the idea is certainly right. You can see his pleasure in discovering things. It goes along with his being a bit puzzled and asking Mrs Klein if she enjoys her work, and trying to construe what is at the heart of psychoanalysis. He is an intelligent child, and he seems to suspect that the discovery of the truth about yourself and the world is a source of some very considerable pleasure, a pleasure which had been relatively unknown to him before. It may have contributed to his fear of being a dunce, for he not only could not learn but could not take any pleasure in learning. These two notes are probably the best statements in her written work of these two aspects of her thinking about integration and about splitting-and-idealization. Taken together they describe the developmental stages that she envisaged, to which the primal splitting-and-idealization is a precondition of development. This split had gradually to be brought together as persecutory anxieties diminished and finally was given a very strong impetus for integration under the pressure of depressive anxiety.

With that discussion in hand, it might be useful to examine the Monday session in detail.

This is the 46th session, Monday:

Richard presented a very different picture. [*The Sunday session had ended with his golden shoes and her lovely hair.*] 'He was lively, but over excited and his eyes were very bright. He talked constantly and incoherently, putting many questions without waiting for an answer, was restless, continuously, in a persecuted way, watching passers-by, and apparently quite incapable of listening to any interpretation. Mrs Klein interpreted there was no response. He was clearly in a state of strong manic excitement and much more openly aggressive, even directly towards Mrs Klein, than he had been for a long time. He said at once that he had brought the fleet and was planning a big battle. The Japanese, the Germans and the Italians were all going to fight the British. (He suddenly looked worried.) He asked Mrs Klein what she thought about the war situation but went on talking without waiting for an answer. [*It seems at this time the war situation was impressing itself upon him.*] He said he felt very well indeed, there was nothing more the matter with him. He had been writing to his friend Jimmy who was the second most important person in his game – Richard himself being the most important – about plans for battle against Oliver. Then he put out the fleet. The British were stronger than all the others together and were stationed behind rocks, represented by Mrs Klein's handbag and clock. [*This is again a very good indication of the nature of his mania, how it was connected with sleeping with his mother on the one hand and Mrs Klein seeing him on the Sunday on the other, how much he felt he really had these big indestructible objects as his armaments.*]

Suddenly the Italians appeared, but soon turned tail. Other enemies started to fight but one hostile destroyer after another was blown up. Richard said, while putting them aside, 'They are dead'. [*This putting aside of the dead had happened before.*] A small British destroyer fired at a German battleship and at first was supposed to have sunk her; then Richard decided that she had surrendered and the destroyer brought her back. In between, he repeatedly jumped up, looked out of the window and watched children. He knocked on the window to attract their attention, made faces at them, but quickly withdrew behind the curtain; he behaved similarly toward a dog; he said of a young girl that she looked silly. He was particularly interested in all the men who passed by ... He looked at Mrs Klein, admired the colour of her hair, touched it quickly, also fingered her frock to find out what it was made of. Then he spoke of a 'funny' old woman who had walked past the house. When he had started the fleet play he made, as usual the noise of engines, something like chug, chug, chug. He interrupted himself and said, 'What is this? I have now got it in my car.'

After having sunk the enemies' fleets, Richard suddenly became 'tired' of playing and put the fleet aside. He took the pencils out and at once put the yellow pencil into his mouth, biting it hard. Then – which was unusual – he pushed the pencil into his nostril and into his ear, put his finger to one nostril and made various sounds. At one point he said the noise was like the whirlwind in *The Wizard of Oz* which blew Dorothy away, who was a nice girl; she did not die as a result of the whirlwind. Meanwhile he asked Mrs Klein whether she liked his light-blue shirt and his tie. [*That is another indication of the light-blue mummy and getting all mixed up with her*] but did not seem to expect an answer. He took out his handkerchief to wipe his nose, although he did not need it, but he looked at it and said 'My mucous hanky'. [*He must have said this with some sort of affection.*]

Mrs Klein interpreted that he particularly wished her to admire his shirt and tie, which also stood for his body and his penis, because he felt that he was mucous, actually had poison inside; with it he meant to attack the internal parents and they would retaliate with poisonous attacks on him. Mrs Klein also pointed out that by biting the pencil he had attacked and taken in Daddy's hostile penis and that the noises Richard had made went on inside him, he had said he had heard the chug, chug, chug, inside his ear. In his mind the fleet battle went on internally and these fights would injure not only himself but the internal good mummy, just as the whirlwind blew away the nice Dorothy. This meant he was the magician who had arranged all these battles. [*That is an interpretation intended to stop the mania cold, by warning him that he is carrying out something that is dangerous to his internal situation, of the anxieties implied about Dorothy and of the chug-chug going on inside him. Such an interpretation has too much of an action in it rather than a communication. Richard is in no mood to be put off in this way.*]

Richard had been grimacing, biting the pencil violently and asked whether Mrs Klein would mind if he broke it or bit it through. Not waiting for an answer he asked whether Mrs Klein liked her son. He was scribbling his name all over a page, nearly illegibly, and then covered it up with further scribbles'. [*Further evidence that the interpretation had not yet touched him.*] Mrs Klein interpreted that, in the fleet play, the little destroyer fighting the battleship stood for Richard fighting against his mother. (Richard had got up, was running about not listening at all and continuing to make noises.)

Mrs Klein suggested that the 'silly' Mummy-fish which in the drawing of the previous day had got in the way of the torpedo and stood for Mrs Klein who exposed herself to his attacks, was today represented by the 'silly' girl who passed by. He had recently expressed his aggressiveness more openly and had said today that he had written to Jimmy his plans for an attack on Oliver. He wished to be able to have an open and external fight. [*Here she brings in the theme of externalization.*] When he had decided to attack Oliver he had said he was happy (33rd session) and had hated his pretence of friendliness when he loathed his enemy. But he nevertheless had expressed his hate by secret attacks, by 'big job' – the scribble hiding his name and the fleet battle which he felt was going on internally represented by the chug-chug in his ear. His jealousy of his parents, and now of Mrs Klein and her husband or her son, again and again stirred up his hate; and since he felt he had taken them into his inside, he could not help feeling that the fight went on internally and not only externally. [*She has got down to work with his duplicity, and his contempt for the object that he feels he can possess and control. This really touches him.*]

Richard had been sniffing and swallowing. [*That is, he had become rather more anxious and hypochondriacal.*] Mrs Klein reminded him that two days ago he had said that his mucus

was running down into his stomach; he felt he was attacking the enemy parents inside his stomach with poisonous
mucus which also stood for poisonous urine and faeces. He
expected that they would do the same to him. This internal
battle would make him feel he had dead people inside him,
whom he could not put aside like the fleet, and he was particularly worried about the injured or dead mummy inside,
represented by the 'silly' fish or by Dorothy in *The Wizard of
Oz*, blown away by his own faecal whirlwind.

Richard, while Mrs Klein was interpreting, had begun to
draw a battleship.

The mania is under control by now. The first interpretation
that she made to him, which in many ways was substantially
correct, did not get at the duplicity and the contempt for his
object which is such an important part of the mania, that is,
the triumph over Mummy and Mrs Klein whom he feels he has
seduced and brought under control. He was sleeping in Mummy'
s bed and he was having Mrs Klein on the Sundays and everything was under his control, as he felt with the pencils in his
hand that he could kill Hitler. He could be Hitler, as it were, for
if you could kill Hitler you could take his place. This seems to
be a very important illustration about the problem of mania and
the problem of interpreting mania. When Mrs Klein interpreted
to him something equivalent to 'How can you treat your mother
like that?', that is really the question that needs to be answered,
that you can indeed treat your mother like dirt, when your internal mother has become dirt by yielding herself to your seduction
and has thereby demonstrated to you that she does not know the
difference between good and bad herself. This is the substance of
this session, and the substance of his mania, which had its origin
in the previous session, a Sunday session. He felt very strongly
that Mrs Klein was utterly swept away by his admiration of her
silver dress and lovely hair and on Monday expects her to admire
his light-blue shirt. The two of them would be cohabiting in
mutual idealization in the same way he and his mother are by
their sleeping in the same room.

It is a very beautiful illustration not only of Richard in his more
destructive and more violent moods but is also an illustration

of how ineffectual an interpretation can be in relation to mania when it does not get at this nub: the contempt of the object and the contempt in the transference for this Mrs Klein, whose bag and clock were the rocks behind which he could hide and attack everybody.

CHAPTER TEN

Tenth week: sessions 53–59

The composition of intolerance to frustration – review of the ten weeks' work

Since this week rather marks the beginning of the end, it might be useful to take stock of what has happened in the 21 months of the treatment so far. It is a week fairly full of suffering, mainly related to the father being in 'X' and Richard being expelled from his mother's bedroom. But it is also filled with the beginning of his suffering about the termination.

There is a very interesting episode about the catching of the 'salmon parr' and the killing of it. Richard has an authentic response of anxiety and guilt on the one hand and regret about it. It links with the episode where for a moment he was confused between the three women who were present at the river when he caught the parr and the three 'silly' women who were outside the consulting room in the session with Mrs Klein. She takes it up only in terms of anxiety about killing mummy's baby, which is certainly correct. It comes up again in a more reparative form in the material about the kitten, as evidence that he has also good feelings towards other children/mummy's babies. Mrs Klein does not however take up his identification with this little salmon parr, feeling himself to be the baby who is hooked away from the mummy. It comes up in the drawings about the mother fish

and all the little fishes, and the bait that is being let down into
the water. The feeling is unmistakeable that one of the baby fish
is going to take the bait and be hooked away. Perhaps she does
not pay much attention to that aspect because of still being a bit
preoccupied with the genital conflict and the castration anxiety.

In the Thursday session the central issue is one of jealousy
and anxiety about the other men in Mrs Klein's life, starting with
Mr Klein, her son, grandson, Mr Smith, Mr Evans, the 'Grumpy
old Gentleman', the 'Bear'. Her men are all objects of extreme
suspicion and jealousy. This central problem, which she has
focused on very sharply, is his distrust of his mother, how easily
she turns bad in his mind. He is not able to split-and-idealize and
keep the good and bad aspect of his objects well separated from
one another. The moment the combined object is formed, the
moment the mother comes together with the father, the moment
the breast is apprehended as coming together with the nipple to
form a combined part-object, it becomes an object of paranoid
mistrust. Cook and Bessie are going to poison him. Father is felt
to be a Hitler father, a greedy father who takes the good things
and puts in the bad stuff instead. It comes out for instance in
his saying he was drinking 'little job' when Mrs Klein saw him
drinking two bottles of lemonade. It comes out in the drawing
with the anti-aircraft gun shooting at the dot in the middle of
the circle (43). She recognizes this as the breast, but does not pay
attention to the dot as nipple at this point. She is however very
much focused on the problem of his mistrust of his object and
its relation to his own trickiness. The 'Larry-the-Lamb' material
comes up again in relation to the tricky 'Chinese Ambassador' in
the aeroplane that was being struck by lightning. The duplicity
of this Larry-the-Lamb is dealt with mainly in Freudian form,
of projection as attribution: being tricky himself, he is naturally
prone to attribute trickiness to his objects.

In 1941 Mrs Klein was not yet actually utilizing her concept
of projective identification. Perhaps more important, she was
not equipped for seeing the material at a part-object level, as a
combined object. She is very aware of the coming together of the
parents, their forming this combined object. But she is not able
to link that with the increasing attention to the breast material
in the transference, manifest for instance in his regular drinking

from the tap at the beginning of the session, or drinking the two bottles of lemonade and expressing it as 'little job'. The strong emphasis on greed and urgency seems to indicate that the material is coming to the infantile level of relationship with the breasts. This rather strengthens Richard's omnipotent trends and his wish to be able to control his object, as in the material about his playing with the rope, putting it between his legs, being God with the lightning in control of the whole situation. One can see very clearly in the material that what is driving him now increasingly is his anxiety about the ending of the analysis, of being hooked from his object like the little fish, of his objects being taken away from him by the daddy, who is going to fill the mummy with all the new babies. Mrs Klein's emphasis on the role of frustration in her reconstruction of his babyhood is not one-sided. As always she insists that the developmental difficulty is not due to frustration alone. The ways in which the child experiences frustration, for instance as a punishment for his own aggression, or as a result of making his object bad in some way, through projections, cause the frustration to be not just a deprivation but a persecution.

In addition to the environmental situation pressing on him this week, that is the father's presence in 'X' and Richard's expulsion from the bedroom, there is also hanging over their heads this difficult issue about the Sunday session. Mrs Klein is now fairly convinced that it is having a disturbing rather than a helpful effect upon Richard. She tries to leave it up to him but finds he can not make a decision not to have any more Sunday sessions. It is very striking how they have impinged upon him. Mainly he has felt that he was being allowed to exploit and empty and damage his object with his greed. This tended to mobilize quite excessive quantities of depressive anxiety, but also insecurity, for an object that would allow him to do this might also allow rivals to do the same. If he is allowed to parasitize and empty the breasts, what was daddy doing down at the genitals, and what were the other babies doing inside the mother? It is very noticeable this week that there has been some lessening of Richard's hostility and fear of children on the road, even toward the little red-haired girl who asked him if he were Italian. It might be because he is more preoccupied with the adult figures and less with the children, but also because he has moved 'up' in his transference, less preoccupied with the genital and abdominal contents of the mother, as reflected generally in his undersea drawings. He is now much more preoccupied with the breast situation and with the combined-object.

This progress is shown most clearly in the Thursday session, which is extremely intense:

> Richard went to meet Mrs Klein much nearer her lodgings than usual. [*As a rule when he was early he waited either in front of the playroom or met Mrs Klein at the corner of the road, which meant he walked for a minute or two with her.*] He was very excited because he had brought her a letter from his mother, asking her to make two changes next week, so that he could spend more time at home with his brother who was coming on leave. He also asked Mrs Klein what she had decided about the Sunday hours after the following Sunday, after which his father would have returned home. Richard was delighted when Mrs Klein replied that she would change the times and would not see him on Sundays after the next one. He was obviously relieved about Mrs Klein's decision. He put his arm swiftly round her shoulder, saying that he was fond of her. He suddenly remembered that he had left the fleet at home; he said he had meant to bring it. [*Usually when he did not bring the fleet he gave definite reasons for having left it behind, or merely said he did not feel like bringing it.*] Richard noticed, after a quick glance, that Mr Smith was coming along the road and would therefore have met Mrs Klein by herself if Richard had not been with her. Richard pointed this out casually, saying 'There is Mr Smith', but went on at once talking about the change of sessions [*presumably to absorb her attention*].
>
> Mrs Klein, when they arrived at the playroom, referred to what Richard had said recently about her meeting Mr Smith and that Richard, by waiting for her at the corner, might have wanted to find out whether she met Mr Smith sometimes on the way to the playroom. He had repeatedly, and again on the previous day, expressed his jealousy and suspicion about Mrs Klein going to the grocer's and to Mr Evan's shop. [*The mother taking her genitals to the daddy's genitals to get her supplies from him.*]

Richard looked searchingly at Mrs Klein and asked whether Mr Evans was very fond of her, and whether he 'gave' her many sweets. Mrs Klein interpreted his jealousy of every man whom she met or might have known in the past. He was still jealous of Mr Klein although he knew he was dead. But when he referred to him as if he were alive, this not only meant he felt Mrs Klein still contained him, but that Mr Klein stood also for all the men with whom Mrs Klein in the present might have sexual relations. He also seemed to be very suspicious of Mummy in this respect.

Richard sat down at the table and asked for the pad and pencils. Mrs Klein discovered that she had left the pad at home. [*In the earlier session she had brought a yellow pad, having been unable to get a white one and he had been terribly disappointed. The next day she had a white one and he was thrilled.*] She said she was sorry and Richard tried to control his feelings and said he was going to make his drawings on the back of earlier ones. He first drew three flags next to one another – a swastika, the Union Jack, and the Italian flag – and then sang the National Anthem. Then he drew a few musical notes and sang a tune to these notes; he wrote 3 + 2 = 5 but did not give any associations. Then he began scribbling on another page, making dots with quick, angry movements and in between he wrote his name and hid it again under the scribbles. Now his anger and sorrow which he had been trying to restrain had become quite apparent, both in his movements and in his facial expression. He looked very much changed – white and suffering – and it was clear that his anger about Mrs Klein not having brought the pad was coupled with misery. [*That is very important. He was miserable for being so overwhelmed by anger toward her.*]

Mrs Klein interpreted that her not bringing the pad was felt by Richard as if the good Mummy at that moment had turned into the hostile and bad one who was also allied with the hostile Daddy – now Mr Smith. This was shown in the drawing of the flags; the British flag, representing himself, was squeezed in between the hostile German and Italian flags. [*A slightly strange idea! She is really interpreting that the mother squeezes him in between the hostile men, Mr Smith/*

Klein/ Evans.] Richard also felt that Mrs Klein and Mummy had turned hostile towards him, because when he was frustrated and did not get enough milk and love and attention from Mummy, he soiled her secretly with his urine and faeces; therefore in turn he expected her to frustrate him as a punishment. [*Lacking the concept of projective identification, she must attribute persecution to expectation of retaliation. She can not suggest that with his urine and faeces he splits off a hostile part and projects it into her in order to be rid of the misery he feels about being so hostile.*] 'Mrs Klein also suggested that when he was jealous of men in connection with her – Mr Smith, the grocer, Mr Evans – be tried to believe that they were nice. At the same time he suspected them of being insincere and 'rascals' towards her and towards him. The 'nice' Mrs Klein and the 'light-blue' Mummy also seemed in his mind to be sweet, but he could not trust them either; as soon as they withheld love and goodness – now the pad – they turned into enemies. [*This is the focus of the work now.*]

Richard had been scribbling angrily, spoke for a moment like Larry-the-Lamb, but quickly returned to making angry noises. Meanwhile he had been sharpening all the pencils, and, swiftly, with a glance to see whether Mrs Klein saw him do it, he bit the green pencil, which had often stood for mummy (and which, so far, he had not bitten or injured) and put its rubber end into the pencil sharpener, thereby damaging the rubber. [*There is the nipple material.*] He scribbled over Drawing 43 which represented an anti-aircraft gun shooting at a round object and which had been interpreted by Mrs Klein as Richard shooting at Mummy's breast. [*He is shooting in fact at the dot in the middle, the nipple.*]

Mrs Klein interpreted that Richard's biting the pencil and secretly using the sharpener on the rubber end expressed his feeling that he had secretly bitten up and destroyed Mummy's breast as well as soiled it. These feelings came up again every time he felt frustrated. But he also felt every disappointment and deprivation as a punishment for having attacked or destroyed Mummy's breast. [*That is, she is interpreting a circular system of conflict. The more he attacks, the more he experiences deprivations as punishments and retaliations.*] Now he had expressed this in relation to Mrs Klein – the pencil representing her as well as Mummy; he had been careful that she should not see what he was doing to her. [*Again emphasizing the secrecy.*]

Richard went outside [*the claustrophobia*] and noticed a man in the garden on the other side of the road (which was at a distance at which he could not possibly hear what was being said). Richard said anxiously, 'He watches us, don't speak'; then he whispered, 'Please say "go away".' Mrs Klein said this. [*This was her technique; at one point she gives him her penknife, which is a little surprising.*] But since of course the man did not go, Richard went back to the playroom. But even there he walked on tiptoe. He found a quoit on a shelf, threw it against the stools and up to the ceiling. He said under his breath 'Poor old thing'. [*Here is the crucial mixture of his sadism and his depressive concern for the breast.*] When it rolled toward the cupboard (which formerly Richard had closed so that the ball would not fall into it) he took it quickly away [*separating the objects*].

Mrs Klein pointed out that the 'poor old thing' represented her breast and genital, pushed violently against the genitals of various men [*the stools*] – Mr Smith, Mr Evans the grocer – of whom he had been jealous. In that way he meant to punish and illtreat both parents, was suspicious of both and became very sorry for them.

Richard was writing something and read it out in defiant tone: 'I'm going back home on Monday to see Paul. Ha-ha ha-ha, ho-ho-ho-ho. Haw-haw-haw-haw.'

Mrs Klein interpreted that Richard wished to show her that he was pleased to leave her [*the separation situation*] and could turn to Paul, because he felt frustrated by her (not bringing the pad) and jealous, believing that she preferred Mr Smith or Evans to him. But he also wanted to show that he did not care, that he felt triumphant and punished her by deserting her. He might also have had such feelings when he allied himself with Paul against Nurse, standing for Mummy. He had just written 'Haw-haw-haw' which meant that he was like Lord Haw-Haw, of whom he had spoken repeatedly as the worst traitor to this country. Richard felt he was like him if he turned against his parents with secret biting and bombing attacks. [*Mrs Klein has succeeded in improving Richard's splitting-and idealization again.*]

Richard went to the window and looked out. He said under his breath 'Why don't you keep me for two hours every day?'

Mrs Klein asked, did he mean twice daily? Richard replied 'No, two hours at a time.'

Mrs Klein interpreted that he had been deeply upset because she did not bring the white pad, which stood for his good relationship with her and for her good breast, and yesterday had been linked with the Milky Way...

The breast material has come absolutely into the forefront in spite of the fact that Richard was expelled from his parents, bedroom and the complication of the Sunday session which had aroused a lot of castration anxiety, and resentment at the genital level. The movement of the transference is toward the breast and the central anxiety is one of being hooked away, deprived, being weaned prematurely (he was weaned to the bottle at a few weeks as a baby). The feeling that this weaning was a conspiracy between nipple and breast or between father's penis and mother's genitals to fill her with babies who would take the breast away from him, is connected with his fear and hatred of other children. This is in a sense his main symptom, his main incapacity for life. It makes him unsocialized and unable to go to school.

It might be useful to spend a little time in trying to see where the ten weeks of work has brought the analysis. This Thursday session, the 56th, seems a bit of a watershed, for Richard has reached a fairly intense experience of the breast. The first thing to note is the way in which the material has changed. In this week the fleet play is more authentic than ever before, experienced no longer either as a diversion to keep Mrs Klein busy nor as a device for controlling his objects omnipotently to make a happy family. The fleet play gets very much at the heart of the conflict of possession of the object in the rivalry and ambivalence towards the object. On the Friday a terrific confusion arises about what is happening, who is fighting whom. The empire drawings which were quite important at one time are fading out now, tending to be replaced by more pictorial drawings, the air combat ones, those of the planes being struck by lightning and the railway drawings with their interesting names. He gives Mrs Klein a lot of material verbally now, transference material in every way, relating directly to her. He is seldom fighting the interpretations, but rather thinking about them and even amending them and improving them sometimes, as when he made a link about the searchlights ('You search, don't you?'). He goes out of the room much less and is very little occupied with those intrusive elements in this peculiar playroom, which earlier on had disturbed him so much and had been used quite a lot as a diversion. The stools seem to have become a fairly stable part of the equipment of representation. His dreams are coming at fairly regular intervals, not very frequently, but most of them are fairly pithy and the last one, the one about his trial, seems to be particularly important for highlighting the problem of his duplicity and trickiness (the Larry-the-Lamb material). The undersea drawings, which have related mainly to his intrusion inside the mother, and to hypochondria – his catching cold and his fear of being poisoned, also seem to have made an advance. The whole phase that was concerned with intrusion inside the mother (the submarines, the fishes, the starfishes, attacking the father's penis inside the mother, the fear of being trapped, the claustrophobia, the hypochondria connected with it) has been rather left behind. What replaces it is preoccupation with the genitality of the situation and the castration anxiety which Mrs Klein probably took up excessively, for it gradually became a bit clearer that it was not the genitality itself that caused the trouble. Confusion of zones of the mouth, genital, anus, of bombing and biting, began to highlight Richard's helplessness. Dependent material came forward and now, by the tenth week, it had begun to sort itself out, with this strong emphasis on his oral needs, his hunger, his intolerance of frustration and the ease with which frustration of his oral needs gives rise to distrust of his objects and to secret attacks.

The whirlwind progress of this treatment up to the tenth week seems to be the consequence of both patient and analyst being under terrific pressure, knowing they have only four months. One must not look upon it as therapeutic triumph attributable either to the obvious brilliance of Mrs Klein's work or of Richard's intense co-operation. It is better understood in terms of the very great flexibility in the analytical method and process. Whatever is available is made use of in the same pattern, whether in a session, a month, or ten years. The same fundamental pattern of the process is made use of but, as Mrs Klein emphasizes repeatedly, one cannot expect that reaching this transference situation with her in ten weeks can possibly have the same therapeutic significance for the child as the same process having been worked through over and over again in, say, three years. The transference has reached this point in rather a headlong way but nothing has been worked through. Mrs Klein is very worried about whether, at the end of four months, he will be left with anything that can not immediately be thrown away, as for instance, his threat to go to Paul, ha-ha-ha. In the next six weeks Mrs Klein will be seen to try very hard to consolidate some foothold in relation to his capacity for depressive feelings.

CHAPTER ELEVEN

Eleventh week: sessions 60–65

The clinical manifestations of splitting processes and the structural meaning of integration, with special reference to the concept of ambivalence

This is a week that presents us with a very interesting problem about analysis, the one that arises from Richard's father becoming ill. It produces a very different response from the time when his mother was ill, which threw him into something of a panic and an attempt to split and idealize in a very frantic way. Richard's father's illness occurred dramatically and it seems that Richard found him collapsed, presumably from a heart attack or some aspect of heart disease. It came after the Monday session which had the fascinating material about Mr and Mrs Bluebottle and Richard's savage attack on the moth, following which he became very persecuted. He was very anxious when Mrs Klein referred to it as a beetle instead of a moth and all this was in the context of his fear of thunderstorms.

That session was very dominated by the prospect of Richard's father, who had been staying in X, going away again, and it was still, as the previous week had been, under the sway of the Oedipus complex, although at a more pregenital level than Mrs Klein was inclined to think. However, when his father then became ill, Richard developed a psychotic depressive state in miniature. Its manifestation was focused on his knife, the same knife with which he had attacked the moth. It now became virtually a suicidal instrument. He put it in his mouth, he hit his teeth with it, he pointed it at himself and Mrs Klein was worried enough to warn him of the danger.

This seems to be a very important analytical problem that has to do with questions of omnipotence. Analysis functions not only to bring up infantile problems from the depths but also to stir and intensify them. If, when infantile problems are stirred up in this way, they then encounter fortuitous events in the outside world which set up a terrible reverberation, the potentiation of omnipotence can give rise to very dangerous problems. This is, I think, illustrated very dauntingly here. Richard acts very concretely, as if his knife had got into his father's heart. There is a bit of material later where he is poking around in the water tank in the kitchen and he says, 'This is the inside of my father's heart'. He is not poking round with his knife just then, but with the poker, yet it certainly links clearly with the material two days previously when he was scratching the poles of the tent, equipment belonging to the Girl Guides, and later on going about with an axe and hitting the flue of the stove. Mrs Klein is worried and lets him off rather easily, perhaps slightly conspiring with his manic-reparative tendencies (clearing out the soot). But she did not get away with it because he became extremely persecuted on the Saturday when he discovered that the splashing of water on Friday and Saturday had caused spots of rust to appear on the stove. Mrs Klein had to clean them off for him.

We cannot suppose that Richard drove his father into his illness. It functions as a fortuitous event that meshes with his outburst of savage omnipotence with his penknife and the moth in the context of the thunderstorm and his fear of it. How has Mrs Klein taken this up with him and what sort of conceptual equipment did she have at that time for dealing with such a thing? One can see that her attitude towards omnipotence at this point in the 1940s was still very closely linked to Freud. Omnipotent wishes, the omnipotence of word and gesture, magic – these seem to be her conceptual tools, in spite of the fact that she has been taking up with him problems of internalization, of internal persecution, attacks on his internal objects and the mother's internal babies.

It clearly implies that at the time of this clinical work she still hedged the question of omnipotence and the concreteness of the experience of psychic reality. She speaks about the guilt and anxiety as manifestations of his imagination and his feelings 'as if' he had done such and such. It seems characteristic of her work after the 1946 paper on splitting and projective identification that the 'if-ness', the distinction between phantasy and reality which characterizes Freud's work, tends to disappear. It is replaced by an insistence on the concreteness of psychic reality. Objects are really damaged in the inner world; they really become persecutory; they really do have to be repaired; no manic pretence of doing it really accomplishes the job. The later work, in this way, places acknowledgement of psychic reality at the centre.

Very interesting things happen in this week as a consequence of Mrs Klein's handling of the suicidal impulse that was acted out with the knife. One of the things she notices is that there is an increased splitting-and-idealization in his relationship to her, reversed at this point, not by her being the bad one and his Mummy being the good one, but the other way round. Mrs Klein is the dark-blue mummy in one session and the light-blue mummy in the next session. But she also notices that he is only listening to half her interpretation. A fascinating observation! He is in a dreamy, far-away state while she interprets his depressive anxiety and his guilt, but as soon as she begins to interpret his reparative tendencies he is right there. It is very amusing that he should ask her the question 'what are you thinking of?' because you can see he is immediately in projective identification with the object and carrying out the analytical reparative work.

The interesting and important thing about her being the dark blue mummy and then the next session the light-blue mummy is that it brings home very clearly the integration of the experience. Richard is now beginning to give evidence, in a quite remarkable way for the eleventh week of an analysis, of his ability to experience the oscillation in the quality of his object, from being good to being bad, it becomes so rapid that he is almost able to feel ambivalent. Ambivalence is a term that seems to be used very loosely by Mrs Klein. It was not used so loosely by Freud and certainly not by Abraham in particular, who considered the achievement of the experience of ambivalence the beginning of mental health. It is not experienced where the love and hate for the object are kept very wide apart. For Richard to be able to experience his love and his hate for Mrs Klein, his trust and his distrust, his pleasure to be there yet his hatred of coming, so closely together that they just oscillate back and forth, is very akin to experiencing his ambivalence itself. It would make one think that his progress in the analysis is fairly substantial at this point in terms of the experience of his emotionality. On the other hand, one has to look at how little feeling he seems to have about his father's illness. Apparently, from the evidence, he is really quite unable to feel this event as a problem of the potential loss of a loved object either for himself or for his mother and brother. His dramatization when he reported the matter initially is pretty thin emotionally. When Mrs Klein does bring him more into contact with his feelings they are almost entirely primitive infantile ones towards his father as a part-object, which then gets tangled up with the killing of the moth.

However, the infantile area of his emotionality is coming through very strongly now; he tells Mrs Klein that he loves her in the Saturday session and it is true, not at all like his seductiveness at the beginning or his manic admiration of her silvery dress or her hair; love seems to gush out of him when he suddenly kisses the drawing he made and kisses the breast. It is as authentic in its love as his attack on the moth was authentic in its hate. So the work of carefully analysing the Larry-the Lamb aspects, his insincerity, duplicity, trickiness, seems to be paying off at this point, in the limited area of his infantile emotionality. However, it is important to notice the paradox that there is not by any means an accompanying improvement in the emotional depths of his relationships at a more mature level, as manifest by his reaction to his father's illness.

This paradox is perhaps clarified by the drawing of Mrs Klein with the big V and the little V for Victory. Children's drawings in analysis, especially those of latency children can be quite uninteresting in their manifest content. The classical thing is patterns. There are almost always interesting items in the drawing, but hidden so carefully from the child himself that their presence in the drawing is clearly unconscious. It requires a great deal of looking, just sitting and gazing, before any hidden meaning might suddenly leap out from the page. If the child will let you, it is very important to watch the process of drawing to see the sequence in which things are done and also to be gazing at previous drawings, especially those that seem in any way related. There was probably no secret intention in putting drawings nos. 54 and 55 on the same page, but one of the things that they illustrate is the strong artistic similarity they bear to one another – as, for instance, in different periods of Picasso's work – the realistic drawings of the Blue Period and suddenly the Cubism. Drawings nos. 54 and 55 have a very strong relationship to one another, one abstract and the other representational. The two smaller circles of the railway drawing turn into the head and breasts of the portrait of Mrs Klein. The railways have a link back to the recent series of railway drawings, but the circle also has a reference back to the anti-aircraft gun which was firing into the air in drawing 43, which in turn, is the converse of 42 and 47, of the lightning striking the aeroplane.

One can begin to see that the same phantasy has many different iconographic representations, just as Richard has often shifted his play representations. In retrospect, it gives strong hints that all of the station drawings with the trains going through between the two stations, had to do with, on the one hand, the breasts and the baby between the breasts, as well as the penis going into the vagina. The conflict between the two situations was most clear in drawing 50 where the father was coming through in one direction and Richard coming through in another. Who was going to get to the station first? Also the baby's victory was indicated when Mr Klein was to go away, sobbing. Previous drawings of this sort can now be seen as representations of the mother's body, the father's penis as a train, the baby's tongue also as a train. The confusion about which is going to get to the breasts and which to the genitals can be seen by juxtaposing the anti-aircraft gun drawings with the lightning-striking-the-plane drawings. Being down below, shooting up at the breasts has something to do with the feeling that the bad penis gets into the vagina and shoots poison into the breasts. This conflict and confusion is temporarily resolved in drawing 55 when the transference to Mrs Klein and her body produces the two V's for Victory, the big victory up above for the baby at the breast and the little victory down below for the daddy at the genital. This horizontal splitting has enabled the baby Richard to feel that what he is getting at the breast is protected either way, or at least not disrupted, by whatever the father is doing down at the mother's genital.

This week also raises a technical problem, about answering questions. Richard asks Mrs Klein why she has not brought the old folder for the drawings and she says she got it wet. He asks what she did with it, and she says she salvaged it. In the note, she says this is contrary to her technique, that is, in so far as it was a reassurance against his suspicion of her Austrian origins. She might explain about its getting wet. Probably the urgency of the countertransference situation, related to the shortness of time, and Richard's frightening playing with the knife on the Tuesday pressed her towards reassuring him. It is very convincing that her response was experienced by him as reassurance and that it had an effect of splitting the transference at that point. Ordinarily one would not have thought that it would be a very impressive piece of reassurance at that time when everyone was salvaging everything. Nonetheless she is right in thinking that it was a reassurance to him in the face of his distrust of her, thinking of her as foreign, admiring her jacket and asking if they wear such colourful jackets on the continent. Since he is still keenly aware of her foreignness and very distrustful of her, it does stand as reassurance and immediately the girl with the curly hair who happens to be passing by, looks like a monster. Why should giving a reassurance about this particular item immediately bring such splitting? The point she makes about it is a very cogent one. The reassurance that brings about this increased splitting-and-idealization does not represent an increase in trust but quite the contrary. It represents a loss of trust in her as if Richard were to think 'If she were honest, she would not have to say how honest she is.'

The note 1 on page 267 raises important questions about integration. There is a great deal of evidence in the material to indicate the coming together of the split in Richard's object and of his being very close to ambivalence and the pain of it. Mrs Klein tended to distinguish between 'integration of the self' and 'synthesis of the objects', but it is not clear what distinction is implied by employing the different words. 'Adequacy' of splitting-and-idealization implies psychological distance between split parts of the self or objects. In excessive splitting, for instance, the fragments might be at such a distance that they have no knowledge of one another; or they can be at a lesser distance where they have knowledge but are not able to communicate with one another; or they can be at a still lesser distance where they can begin to communicate but not influence one another; or they can be so close together that one dominates the other; or so fixed as to become indistinguishable from one another. This is probably the meaning that Mrs Klein wishes to infuse into the concept of integration which is otherwise a very loose and airy one. In Richard's material a fairly concrete and precise application of the concept to the clinical phenomena is possible, both as regards the splits in his self and in his objects. The concrete clinical application of concepts of structure which the 1946 paper were to make possible are all adumbrated here. Other dimensions are hinted at, such as planes of splitting – up and down, front and back, inside and outside. The degree of sadism of the splitting process seems to determine the depressive price for its reparation.

All these lines of development are hinted at in various notes. Thinking about splitting processes in this very concrete way is extremely difficult if one is still hedging about psychic reality in its absolutely concrete sense. It requires an immense shift in one's view of the world to think that the outside world is essentially meaningless and unknowable, that one perceives the forms but must attribute the meaning. Philosophically, this is the great problem in coming to grips with Kleinian thought and its implications. It is only from that point of view that the depressive position acquires the concreteness and the hardness as a concept that makes it an invaluable tool for understanding clinical phenomena. Do people really suffer because they have really damaged their internal objects? In this week there is the beautiful example of the incident about the moth on Monday and the father's illness on the Tuesday. One can see that the father's illness has had an impact on Richard that stands very specifically in relation to this killing of the moth the previous day. Pointing the knife towards himself and hitting his teeth with it had real suicidal significance and were later clarified when he spoke of probing his father's heart (note II, page 304, 61st session).

CHAPTER TWELVE

Twelfth week: sessions 66–71

The role of interpretation in the therapeutic process

Richard returns to playing with the toys for the first time in two months. Mrs Klein has some notes at the end of the session which are of great technical importance. Just to recall the setting: Richard's father is ill and Richard is travelling back and forth between Y where his family is living and X where the analysis is taking place, travelling on the bus. He has started living at the Wilsons, which he does not like. He seems to be managing quite admirably and is rather proud of himself, 'doing his bit'. In connection with his father's illness, he certainly is trying to spare his family. In that way he contributes to holding the analysis and the family rather separated from one another in his mind, which Mrs Klein seems to realize more fully now and states it quite clearly in one of the notes.

There is some additional technical interference during the week other than the disturbed background setting. The first is the somewhat gratuitous information Mrs Klein gives Richard on Tuesday about his very limited breast feeding and early weaning. This has a terrific impact on him, which she justifies a bit in her notes on the basis of the mother having neglected to give this information, despite Mrs Klein's request. Why she picks this point to give it, and why she thinks it necessary to give it at all is a bit mysterious and she is rather apologetic about it. The second and third sessions of the week are dominated by the consequences of that information which excites a terrific flurry of distrust in Richard, distrust of mothers, of breasts, of Mrs Klein and his mother's collaboration with her. This is worsened by the end of the week because there is to be a conversation between the two adults the following Monday. Richard is terribly anxious that they are going to discuss his future, particularly the future of his schooling. He begs Mrs Klein to advise his mother to have a tutor and not to be sent to school and then he settles for a small school, clearly quite terrified still of the prospect of going to a big school, which seems to mean a school full of big boys. The anxiety centres on both the size of the boys and the number of them. A bit of material at the end of the Thursday session shows this when he asks Mrs Klein about all the people in X crowding at the top of the hill. It comes up later about the bus. There is something about the 'crowding' in his concept of a big school that stirs his anxiety about there not being enough attention for him or being crowded out of contact with his good object by these big boys. It is very interesting that his immediate response to Mrs Klein's information about his premature weaning was to ask if the mother had given the breast to Paul, then also to daddy. It seems to him immediately that the breast, if it had been taken away, must have been given to somebody else.

Another technical intrusion affecting the week's work, and interfering a bit with his trust, surrounds Mrs Klein's bringing extra toys on Saturday (the little figures). It seems most unusual as she also admits in the footnotes. She usually leaves broken toys and then replaces them at holiday periods but it is a bit peculiar to have done this at the end of the week. Probably the pressure of the approaching ending of the treatment is affecting her technique. She is hoping to be able to make some arrangement with Richard's mother for the continuation of the analysis in the foreseeable future, but this never actually comes about. It is certainly very clear that Richard is getting more and more desperate about it. But on the other hand, it is mobilizing some fighting spirit in him. He speaks with determination about how he is going to return to his home at Z, and to his fort, and how no-one is going to stop him. There is some sort of spirit mobilized in this boy by the restored relationship to his good objects and he is in consequence less confused and less distrustful.

It might be useful to try to dissect the various types of material that run through the week because it can be very instructive to see how the themes they present interact with one another and what themes they seem to isolate. Mrs Klein writes a very interesting note about how children's material shifts back and forth and in a way, settles the problem about the difference between a shifting of representation and a play disruption. Now, this first theme is about jealousy, which becomes focused on Mr Smith and his meeting with Mrs Klein. Richard is monitoring her, jumping out at her, questioning her, having to run out of the house after Mr Smith passes, to see if he could look in. He never notices, as Mrs Klein of course does, that Mr Smith is taller than Richard and would have a somewhat different view into the playroom. Richard is afraid of people knowing what goes on in his thoughts and feelings in the treatment situation and this is related to the theme of Mr Smith that runs through the whole week and is related to the way 'G' for God keeps coming up in the drawings. His anxiety about the daddy monitoring and attacking him is increased because Mrs Klein insists on his genital desires rather than his oral greed, namely his wish to get inside the mummy and take everything.

This theme of his greed emerges more clearly in his repeatedly playing with the money. This is for his bus fare mainly, but there is quite a lot of material that runs through the week about the money in his pocket, his greed for it and handling of it, links with his anxiety about whether he dirtied it when he scribbled on it, the difference between silver and copper money and spinning the two half-crowns as breasts. It links back with the theme of Mr Smith and the radish seeds for which Richard is very greedy. It is not quite clear what these radish seeds are intended to be, although Mrs Klein takes this mainly in terms of genital desires, to have the seed to give babies to mummy as reparation. Probably the radishes are more connected with the nipple. The strawberries have come up as nipples and suggest that Richard is much more concerned with being able to fill the mother with the kind of seeds which would produce the kind of foods he likes to eat. It is through his feminine attachment to Mr Smith that its significance as seeds for babies arises. Another theme is the line of drawings which continue the big and little V for Victory, ending with a drawing of himself and Mrs Klein putting their genitals together. It appears in the figure-of-eight railway track that has a big siding going out of the top and another little siding going into the loop at the bottom. Mrs Klein examined this in terms of Richard's wish to put a big V for Victory up at the breast, not only getting the food but putting his genital near the breast and having some sort of genital/breast gratification.

The fleet play hardly comes into the week except at the beginning. It seems clear that Richard is rather reluctant to bring the fleet. It belongs more and more to his home life with his family which he desires to keep quite separate from the analysis. As the fleet stays at home, in comes the use of Mrs Klein's toys again. It starts very shyly, bringing out the swing which seemed to represent his masturbation. It is extremely interesting that the first thing to come out of her bag is this wretched swing that always started the trouble and the disaster in the earlier toy play. There has not been a word about masturbation for weeks. Mrs Klein apparently did not think it necessary to mention the actual masturbation when she was dealing with the phantasies underlying it. She might very well be right but probably some of Richard's anxieties, feeling spied upon, and his distrust about his mother and Mrs Klein talking together had something to do with the fear that they are exchanging information.

Nevertheless the toys come out and the play scenes that existed in the earlier toy play are reconstituted and disasters occur, but they are much more controlled disasters at this point and the emphasis is very much on survival. Concern about the breast enters into the play in a way in which it certainly did not before. The trains going round in a circle; the two goods trains are watched by the children who are enclosed in a pencil fence and are allowed to watch the breast and seem to enjoy that. The emphasis is again on trying to establish peace and trying to prevent catastrophe by means of equality, shared experience; nobody should have the breast all to himself. This leads to the phantasy of people crowding up on to the mountain. Fear of deprivation brings the bit of material in which Bobby goes down a rabbit hole, a very oral kind of penis that gets into the mother in a greedy way, all part of the disaster. The other part of the disaster is always the rage and this is represented particularly by the landmine drawing which is connected with Richard gritting his teeth, scribbling and malting dots all over the page. When he notices that the dots go through and make dents on the paper below, he tries to fill them in a little bit. These dots become enclosed and become the landmine and then they turn into the strawberries, first three, then two, and four green leaf-babies. Those leaves are very akin in shape to the starfish-babies and the strawberries look very much like undersea mines. Landmine and undersea mine; strawberry leaves and starfish babies; undersea and above surface are still in many ways confused in this material, implying that internal and external situations are still not very well differentiated. But what does come out so clearly is the preoccupation with the nipple. The main theme is delineated by the strawberries and the radishes and the wish to have all these seeds, millions and billions of them, in order to be able to inseminate the mother with the seeds that produce the food for which Richard is so greedy.

Under the sway of the distrust of his mother and Mrs Klein meeting, which is represented by his caricature, Melanie and Henrietta, the old hen and the nasty old woman, how quickly these hostile elements emerge. In spite of that, the feeling of being able to differentiate good and bad, and being able to trust his objects, is certainly very greatly strengthened by in sight into the consequences of his attacks. When he bites the little doll with the red hat, connected with the red haired girl who he said was choked with rage, he does not like the taste. It certainly connects with the blue ink, which is 'light-blue' Mummy, and a bottle of smelly ink connected with Cook and Bessie's poison, the poisoned breast. This is a very clear indication that he understands that the breast becomes bad when he projects something into it. When the nipple, this little red haired nipple, becomes the head-of-a-child bit of Richard that has got into the breast and is felt to be soiling the breast, urinating and defaecating into it, that is what makes the breast turn bad. And the same result is brought about indirectly by projection into the father. Richard begins to comprehend that it is his own badness, the rascal in himself, which gets into the daddy's penis, which then becomes the Goebbels penis, like a rat and like Bobby going after the rabbits. When that rascal penis gets into the mummy that is what spoils her and changes her into the brute, the wicked brute mummy, the breast that can not be trusted, that might be poisoning and speaking German. That whole theme seems very greatly clarified and has strengthened the emotionality of his participation in the transference. When Richard caresses Mrs Klein and tells her he loves her and wants to be her husband – when he grows up, mind you – it is with great feeling and very little seductiveness. The seductiveness does come earlier when he begs her to go to the cinema. His jealousy is behind it and his distrust of what she is doing at night, wishing to keep an eye on her. But at the end of the week when he is worried about her being lonely and talks about how lonely his mother would be if his father died, this brings forward his wish to marry Mrs Klein and his acknowledgement that her husband is really dead. There is some differentiation between the dead Mr Klein in the outside world and the live Mr Klein and his penis inside Mrs Klein. Richard's concern about the end of his analysis is not merely influenced by consideration for his own welfare, but also about Mrs Klein going back to London and the dangers to her there.

These are the themes that come out mainly through the return to play with the toys. Direct interaction with Mrs Klein is very intense now. The other interesting theme is the one about the baby-tank, the cooking stove and its soot. Where did the water run? It had come up as a sequence in earlier weeks: filling up the sink and wanting Mrs Klein to let the water out while he rushed outside to see where the water escaped. This material, with the soot and dirtiness of the water, shows that he is reaching for some understanding about the functions of the parental intercourse in keeping the milk clean and not allowing the urine and faeces of the babies to contaminate the inside of the mother's body. It will come out even more clearly with the dead flies and reaches its resolution in the dream of the Black Island. Mrs Klein notes that he is now regularly drinking water from the tap. He does not seem to use the lavatory much, judging from the text, although he urinated two or three times in an earlier session and in one of the current sessions he speaks of being unable to urinate though wanting to.

In a general way, then, one might say that in the drawings Richard is clarifying the problem about the breasts and nipples and the competition, the big V for Victory at the breast and the little V for Victory at the genital. Separation anxiety and the anxieties about the ending of the analysis are being worked out more directly with Mrs Klein, while the tendency of jealousy and envy to produce disasters and to engender his worst anxieties and despairs are being worked out in the play with the toys. The fleet is staying at home as a way of separating his home life and, in a way, the more mature part of himself, from the infantile transference situation in the analysis. Finally the problem of contamination and preservation of the goodness and purity of the breast is being worked out largely with the stove and 'baby tank'.

At that time Mrs Klein did not have a concept of confusion. Consequently her interpretations tend simply to delineate the separate phantasies and the particular anxieties connected with them without much sorting out. Her concept of the therapeutic process, as she emphasises over and over again in the notes, rested upon the importance of interpreting the immediate material. Where it was coming up thick and fast, as in the play with the toys, her emphasis was always on selecting the most pressing, and by this she meant generally the 'deepest', anxieties that are available to view. She certainly did believe that the interpretation itself somehow diminished the anxiety. While she often organizes the evidence, it is only very occasionally that she makes an interpretation that links themes together. These interpretations seem rather staccato descriptions of separate phantasies, often overlapping, sometimes seeming mutually exclusive, but her feeling was that these phantasies were all existing at the same time, at different levels, and it was the delineation, and, in Freud's sense, the elevation into consciousness that diminished the anxiety. As persecutory anxiety diminished, depressive anxieties were able to come forward. She did not have a concept of persecutory depression. So it is not surprising to see her misunderstand the ice rink material in the second session. Probably that is the one piece of material in the week she may have genuinely misconstrued. Otherwise, one may not agree with all the different phantasies that she sees operative, but one can see what an extraordinary and fruitful imagination she brought to bear, her excellent memory and ability to link the evidence. Her response to the material is almost always interesting, never pedestrian. Her capacity to move from internal to external, from inside to outside, is fairly remarkable. From the therapeutic point of view the sorting of this deep confusion between good and bad in self and objects is a major accomplishment and is bound to make a major difference to his mental health. Already some benefit is in evidence, mainly manifested at this point in the material, but also in his adjustment outside the analysis, being able to travel alone, being able much of the time to be relatively unpersecuted by other children, improved friendliness for people, for instance, his being able to go back to the hotel to visit the people he had left. Previously he could not even say goodbye to them when he left. An improvement appears in his sense of reality and in his regret about his debilitated state. Towards the end of the week he speaks again of his fear of being a dunce and an imbecile and his regret at not playing the piano. It is really very touching evidence of the strengthening of his capacity to experience depressive anxieties.

CHAPTER THIRTEEN

Thirteenth week: sessions 72–77

The relation of ambivalence to the experience of depressive pain

It is rather a beautiful week, influenced on the outside by Mrs Klein meeting Richard's mother and his anxiety about the kind of school she would recommend. Also the question of plans for the possible continuation of the analysis are in the air. His suspicions and anxieties about these issues more or less dominate the first two sessions. Richard's father's illness casts an influence which threads through the week and there is also the problem about staying with the Wilsons which he does not like. He finds Mr Wilson much more authoritarian than he is accustomed to; he is used to being treated as an only child, not stinted of sweets. The Wilsons are a more disciplined family than his own. He finally begs Mrs Klein and his mother to make other arrangements for him, which they do. He is also jealous of John, who is with Mrs Klein in analysis and is older, about fifteen. He probably feels rather pushed aside when John will not take him for a walk with a friend, or will not climb a mountain with him. Then there is a big disturbance in the setting on Friday, when Mrs Klein brings the oranges, which absolutely drives Richard wild with jealousy.

But in spite of these external factors disturbing the situation, the main themes that have developed through the week are coherent in a very impressive way. Mrs Klein is seen working in top gear and in several places pulls things together very definitively. Finally in the Saturday session she reaches her most advanced formulation of his psychopathology by means of the 'baby-tank' material and the killing of the flies.

It is instructive to tease out the themes and to see how they orient themselves to the different kinds of material. He is playing a lot with the toys again this week, especially in the first three sessions, centering on the problem of the disasters. They mainly take the form of the two trains competing, representing himself and his father in competition for the position of the leader, the husband in the family, and, in part-object terms, the fight of the penises inside the mother which Mrs Klein has spelled out very clearly. Again there is not a direct word about masturbation the whole week. On the periphery of the disaster play there are all the themes having to do with people watching each other, expressing Richard's need to try to control everybody in the family in order to keep his own destructive impulses in check. It never quite succeeds but the disasters are more controlled, and somebody always survives. Reparative impulses take the form of a hospital block where damaged figures may be repaired. Mrs Klein plays into that by actually repairing some of the toys for him.

The fleet comes in briefly to express similar themes at a part object level, for the fleet play and the toy play have come together, but also diverge. The fleet play is more preoccupied with the genitals while the toy play clearly now represents the breast, providing milk for the children. The theme of Richard's greed which lies at the root of his destructiveness and his hatred of other children is thus made clearer. The theme of the competitions with the babies inside the mother for possession of the mother's riches, first expressed in the starfish drawings, now comes out very clearly in the play of the giving of milk to the children. First they are allowed to watch the breast, then they are actually given milk and then the thing goes wrong because of the competition between the goods train and the passenger train, that is, the nipple and the penis. It explodes on the Friday because of the intrusion of the oranges. It is very interesting, for Richard acknowledges that he likes neither oranges nor milk, but the infantile meaning of milk and breast arouses his greed and rage.

Richard has not brought any dreams for about six weeks. Next week, the fourteenth, there is a dream, and then in the fifteenth, a real bonanza of them. But Richard is doing a great deal of talking with Mrs Klein and this shows up the transference particularly clearly. It centres on the termination of the analysis and the feelings of abandonment and anxiety at two levels, being deserted by Mrs Klein as analyst, but also as breast. A series of incidents runs through the material, holding her hand, asking her to speak a little German as if she were talking to her husband, wanting to come and see her at her lodgings, asking her if she will ever come and visit his home. Finally in the Saturday session, rather touching material appears in which he expresses his desire to sleep in Mrs Klein's bed, to snuggle up to her, to caress her, to cuddle her, but not to have any genital contact. On this basis, she finally formulated the horizontal splitting, the separation of the breast mother from the genital mother, relating it also to the situation with his nurse and his mother in early times and the difference between the light-blue mummy and the dark-blue mummy. His ambivalence finally emerges towards the figure of the pretty conductress, who says, 'Half fares stand up', which Richard so much resents. She says this when the bus becomes crowded and it is this crowding in on his relationship with his good objects that is the focus of his more persecuted, not paranoid, feelings. These latter were really tied up with his being confused between the good and bad objects.

The splitting-and-idealization has been very well delineated now, with the result that Richard's ambivalence to his object, the internal object, is much more held together but splits again easily. It appears as a split between Mrs Klein and his mother when she does not want him to go swimming and he turns against her briefly. He turns viciously against Mrs Klein about the oranges. He turns against the bus conductress when she says, 'Half fares stand up' but he admits she is very pretty, much prettier in ordinary clothes than in uniform. This very quick oscillation is not between the idealized light-blue Mummy and the black Mummy, the bird with the crown and the faeces dropping out of its bottom, not the malevolent 'wicked-brute', poisonous Mummy, but this dark-blue Mummy who frustrates him, disappoints him, who has the mysterious genital activities that do not include him. The distinction between this bad mummy who frustrates and disappoints him in sexual ways and the malevolent one who is mixed up with the Hitler-penis and Richard's own projected violence and destructiveness is now sharply drawn, mainly thanks to the dream of the trial and the jack-boots with which he was kicking all the buildings down and kicking them up again.

The oedipal theme is a bit in abeyance now, probably partly due to his father's illness and his being like another baby who is being nursed, has two nurses in fact. Even Mr Smith has dropped out a bit, but Mr Klein is very vivid in his mind and he would really like to know what kind of relationship she had had with Mr Klein and what sort of Mr Klein she has inside her. Is she a happy person with a good husband or a good penis inside her, or was it an unhappy relationship? Does she carry round in her a bad Hitler-kind of daddy?

The theme about his fear of children has begun to give way and Richard has begun to look at them with interest. Although he is suspicious and very frightened of them, he can admire a little girl and say she is pretty and looks rather nice. He keenly wishes John to be friendly with him. Along with that, his boastfulness, his provocativeness towards other children and his contempt for them seems on its way to diminishing rather rapidly. This relief from his hatred of other children seems directly related to the murderousness and anxieties expressed in the 'baby-tank' material. For weeks Richard has been drinking from the tap and examining the water tank which he calls a 'baby tank'. He also repeatedly examines the stove and the soot in it, tears up bits of paper to throw into the water, drains out the water into buckets which Mrs Klein has to empty into the sink so he can find out how it runs out of the house. It all gives an impression of systematic research into the metabolism of the mother's body in relation to good and bad substances. How does the mother manage to get rid of all the bad substances that the baby evacuates into her? That problem becomes clearer than ever before on the Saturday, with the killing of the flies. This links back to the incident of his killing the moth and the bluebottles. Clearly, the trouble is not the baby's evacuation into the mother, but that his evacuations have a hostile, destructive intention towards the babies inside her. It is made explicit by his squashing the flies and links with his tearing up the bits of paper, which Mrs Klein had mistakenly interpreted to him as giving babies to the mummy. Later on he tries to share the blame with the father's penis; he says he only killed two of the flies, the pipe killed the others.

This might be a useful point to turn our attention to the matter of Richard's depressive feelings. Early in the *Narrative* Mrs Klein seemed very impressed with Richard's capacity for love, but perhaps mistakenly at that point, because his expressed love for his mother, his wish to protect her from the tramp, his love for the beauty of nature, all turned out to be primarily connected with his concern for his own comfort. His love for the dog Bobby turned out to be related to sexual collusion and the projection into him of his own naughtiness and faecal dirtying. The very possessiveness and controlling nature of his loving was manifest. Now the intensity of his love for Mrs Klein as the breast mother in the transference relationship resists her technique of interpreting, which tends constantly to push things back to his mother and back to the nurse and back to the past. The intensity of his transference attachment to her and the genuine warmth of it is certainly tied up with a very desperate need of her, but the genuineness, the authenticity of it is very instructive in comparison with the vanity, the use of flattery and seductiveness which characterized his earlier relationship to her.

Now this capacity for love is most certainly tied up with an improved splitting-and-idealization of self and object and the overcoming of the paranoid trend that came out most clearly in the Cook-and-Bessie material. His inability to distinguish between malevolent objects and bad objects produced an intolerance to frustration, disappointment or authority. It was epitomized in the dream of the trial which turned out to be a trial for breaking the window, which in fact he had not broken. But he had wanted to break windows on many occasions and in the dream he smashed all the buildings with his jack-boots and then manically kicked them up again. The light-blue mummy who was idealized as a possession has become a much more separate object and therefore stands in a more oscillating or, at times, ambivalent relationship to the dark-blue mummy. This figure is represented in the material mainly by the pretty bus conductress in the blue uniform who says, 'Half fares stand up'.

This achievement of differentiation between malevolent objects, frustrating objects and idealized gratifying objects brings with it the possibility of depressive feelings. A real desire now appears to repair the object for its own sake and not merely to put a stop to the persecution by the damage when it can not be distinguished in its qualities from the malevolent object. Giving babies to Mummy or kicking the buildings up again was part of the defence against persecutory anxieties and was thus manic reparation. When he said to Mrs Klein very early in the analysis that his mother could have plenty of babies, she was not too old, he was quite insincere. But at this point he has a real feeling for babies that comes from some considerable degree of integration of his femininity. This aspect of his personality enters into the sessions now, bit by bit, over the last four or five weeks, sometimes in competition with the mother for the father's penis, which easily turns into homosexuality and contempt for women. His genuine feeling of warmth for babies first came with the kitten material and is seen a bit more this week, a result of this improved contact with his femininity and related capacity to care for babies, he is also able to look at little girls on the street and see one of them as being rather pretty. He is not even being terribly venomous towards his enemy, the little red-haired girl, although she turns up as one of the flies he squashes. His antagonistic feelings towards girls and his thinking of women as haughty or horrid, those women with yellow sputum and the terrible girl with the buck teeth who asked if he were Italian, have simmered down considerably. What does remain is his fear of big boys, for very little of the analytic work has so far thrown any light on this fear.

The depressive feelings that are able to emerge as a result of the improved contact with his femininity and a greater capacity to identify with the mother, seem to show themselves in this one sudden little bit of material in which he said his nurse had died, and died of pneumonia, her milk froze. That seems to come as a consequence of his being terribly sensitive at this point to the slightest rebuff to the emergence of genuine feelings of warmth from him. When Richard asks Mrs Klein to help him stretch by holding his hand, he feels very rebuffed by her, very hurt, very much like the boy who cried wolf – the touchiness of the recently reformed criminal. Having simulated love so often, he is terribly frightened that this genuine love will be misunderstood, undervalued, thought to be the same old falseness. The material about the nurse seems to be an important indicator, in projective form, the pneumonia, the milk freezing, of his own liability to depression now. There was material two weeks before which Mrs Klein did not grasp about the drawing of the ice rink when he said 'ice, ice, ice'. She did not pick up the first time that he was talking about feeling depression as freezing and here is a second reference to it.

As we approach the last few weeks of treatment this particular indication of a growing capacity to experience depressive feelings in their most essential form, as freezing, helps one to gain an idea of why his manic trend was so strong previously. Richard certainly has been brutally controlling with his objects and experienced them as dead objects which needed to be brought to life, like the black car with the many number plates, or the black bar on the fire. The inner feeling of coldness is in many ways the prototype of depressive pain. Richard is beginning to be able to suffer from it, although only in passing, and in the material about the nurse it is projected outward as a result of his feeling rebuffed and wounded by Mrs Klein. His response to depressive feeling is also very much improved. All through these sessions in one little way or another, he is asking Mrs Klein to help him, to hand him things, to empty the bucket. He is very concerned when he jumps from the step and touches her face that he might have hurt her. His whole relationship to her now is a constant appeal for help, which is the central theme of Mrs Klein's little paper about Colette's story in Ravel's operetta. The moment the child who has destroyed everything in rage can cry 'mamma' and ask for help, the reparative process swings into operation in some mysterious way. This ability to ask for help is now really quite established in Richard's relationship to Mrs Klein and it begins to extend to his mother, when, instead of making demands on her, he can phone to ask if she could make other arrangements for him because he does not like staying at the Wilsons.

CHAPTER FOURTEEN

Technical problems related to countertransference

This is a terrible week. Why it is such a bad week is hard to say. Somehow Mrs Klein is not in such close touch with Richard and even loses her temper with him a bit on the Friday. It might be instructive to review the Thursday session in detail to to see what went wrong and why it is a rather heartbreaking session. The theme of the 'baby tank' which began developing five weeks before has become central now. The water tank in the kitchen has become not only the 'baby tank' but the 'milk tank' as well. The very central issue is the killing of the flies and putting them in the milk and whether the milk is dirty and poisonous. In this week Mrs Klein has lost the formulation she found the previous week, the one that seems to be the climax of the treatment. Instead she keeps going back to the problems of castration anxiety and the competition with the father, all of which is quite true, but not central any longer. It is a complicated week. The threat of the ending hangs over the whole procedure and Richard can often hardly bear to think about it. But it is also very complicated in other ways concerning mainly the two bus conductresses, the pretty one who says 'Stand up' and the other one who does not, and the dark-blue uniform.

To the Monday session he brings the weekend dream that he changed analysts, to a dark-blue analyst, the woman in dark blue with her dog named James. When Richard insists on Mrs Klein's prettiness she notes that he was really placating her like an unfaithful lover. It arises again about his tie which was tied for him by a maid at the Wilsons. It is a little difficult to tell what this theme is, but one strongly suspects that his mother was a rather pretty woman. His attachment to her beauty and the infantile attachment to the beauty of the breasts as an aesthetic object, has entered into the treatment in a very powerful way that tends to replace the dichotomy between the light blue mummy and the dark-blue mummy. It has some reference to his looking at the sky and saying that it is light blue, although it is quite clearly cloudy. He says at another point that it is cloudy but it is going to clear although there seems to be every indication that the weather is worsening. The light-blue mummy who gives him this peace and quiet becomes juxtaposed to the disturbing dark-blue mummy, the cloudy sky, the storm breaking over the mountain, the combined object which insists that he stand up, develop and go to school. He does not like the dark-blue uniform on the pretty conductress because it has a masculine quality, representing the beautiful mummy who also has strength and the good penis inside her, related to the nipple. At one point he asks her again, 'What is this part of the breast called?' and she has to tell him again that it is called the nipple. But Mrs Klein keeps forgetting about the good penis and the combined objects and goes back to talking about his fear of the bad penis that makes mummy into the 'brute-mummy'. This seems to upset Richard because he is very keen that they should be in accord as the end approaches. In several sessions he wishes to synchronize their watches and to make sure they are keeping exactly the same time. At another point, he is very affectionate and cuddles her clock. She does note the desire for this unity of mind, although she speaks of it as though it were mainly a defensive process.

It is also present in his wish for her to be the milk maid and he will be the milk man; together they will milk the baby tank. In the face of repeated disappointment at her failure to follow him and after she has lost her temper a bit with him on the Thursday, he is extremely distrustful of her in the Friday session and will not look at her and says, 'Hitler said "my patience is exhausted".' Early in the treatment he had said that one of his main difficulties was that he exhausted his mother's patience by endless questions. Bouts of this behaviour appear, as when he begins asking about the bad dream, questions her about her son, her grandson and what she will do in London, will she be in the heart of London? It is very interesting to see his recovery when he says 'the heart of London', 'Oh, the heart again'.

In fact Richard is working extremely hard and even when he seems to be out of control, the rapidity with which he recovers and shifts his ground to other material seems to indicate that there is a very strong element of dramatization and communication present. At no point is he terribly out of control, but is, rather, terribly in distress. When he is flooding the floor or hitting it with a hammer, or kicking the stools he never once attacks Mrs Klein. He has at other times actually thrown something at her and also abused her verbally. She seems to underestimate the intensity with which he is trying to work with her to evoke a clarification about the 'baby tank' being the same as the 'milk tank' and how the dead flies get into it. This problem appears also with the lobster he has in his suitcase, reminiscent of the 'delicious monster'. But he also attacks it with his knife as he had attacked the moth. Clearly one minute it is a delicious penis, next, it is a horrible, hated penis or a baby.

The Thursday session brings up clearly the element of fear that the analysis will fail. It comes up with the photographs that he wants to take of Mrs Klein, which she allows, and is connected at that point with the photographs of the landscape, one good, the other a failure, which he tears to pieces and puts the black bits in his mouth and spits them out, saying that they are poison. Very clearly this refers to the dead flies and the bits in his mouth. Fear of the analysis failing is very closely related to his fear of being a dunce, of going to school but not being able to learn. He is obviously intelligent and has already learnt quite a lot at school. She tends to think of his fear of school as being primarily a school phobia, a claustrophobic anxiety, and probably underestimates a bit how intense is his competitiveness and how unbearable are failures to him. Let us examine the Thursday session (no. 81).

Richard was again waiting at the corner of the road. He asked whether it was sixteen days until Mrs Klein's departure. In the playroom, he adjusted his watch to her clock. He opened the clock, inspected it, set the alarm going, and went on opening and closing the leather case, also caressing it with his hands. He said that even if his watch was a little slower than others, yet it was 'going its way', and he drew his finger round the face of the watch. [*There is something rather admirable about these sessions, although it is desperate and unsatisfactory in other ways. He wants something from her and is quite determined to get it.*] He said that nobody, and certainly no other watch, could command that it should stop ... [*It was as if he had said to Mrs Klein, 'You may be stopping the analysis, but I'm not. I'm going on even if I have to go on without you.'*] He quickly looked round the kitchen, glanced uneasily at the 'baby tank', and was disturbed because he saw some rust on it. He tried to scrape it off and seemed grateful when Mrs K removed the rust with a brush. [*It is not clear why she does this unless he asked for help, to which she usually responds now.*]

He quickly went back to the table and again looked into the clock to see whether it was still working ... He told Mrs K that he had a secret which she did not know. He had cycled to the end of the road last evening, and had passed her house. Where did the little path at the end of the road lead to? What was Mrs K doing at about 8.45 last evening (which was the time when he had passed her house)? Would Mrs K have been angry if had looked in? He did not wait for answers to any of these questions but went on speaking. He explained that he had borrowed the bicycle the day before and had cycled all over the village. [*Really quite adventurous of him.*] Unfortunately it had been too late to go farther out to the next village as he had intended. [*Connected with his plan to climb a mountain with John and his friend.*] He went on describing his exploit in detail and said it had been fun and he had enjoyed it very much. When he went downhill he made noises to himself, as if he were a bus. [*Containing the dark-blue pretty conductress-mummy.*]

Mrs K interpreted, as often before, that when Richard investigated her clock, this meant looking into her inside and reassuring himself about her still being all right. [*This is the line on which she keeps working.*] The same applied to his looking around the kitchen. Both were connected with his killing the flies on the previous day, the mess he had made in the kitchen, and his fear of the harm he had done in this way to Mrs K. His cycling tour showed that he was less afraid of other children and also served as a means to satisfying his curiosity. Cycling past Mrs K's lodgings meant the exploration of her inside. The little path represented her genital and he wondered where it would lead if he puts his penis – the bicycle – into it. [*Thirst for knowledge or intrusive curiosity?*] He seemed to be less afraid of his penis being a dangerous weapon and could therefore use the bicycle. [*This little path was something like a delivery entrance and he was curious about it, curious about the structure of the mother's body and the connection between the side entrance and what was going on in the main part of the house. In that way the connection between the sexual relationship of the mother to the father's penis and the breast with its supplies and thus the connection between the 'baby tank' and the 'milk tank', is illustrated.*] All this meant that his fear about his hatred and destructive wishes taking effect had lessened. His watch 'going its way' though slowly, stood for the smaller, less potent, but uninjured genital. He seemed to accept that it was only a boy's genital, but he hoped he would be a man in the future. [*This is her desire, to get him into the latency period and quieten him down. One can not blame her.*] Making his watch agree with Mrs K's clock meant that they would understand each other and he could keep her as a friend, also inside him. [*Here she gets at it.*]

Richard, again manipulating the clock, said with strong emotion, 'Must we two part?' He went outside, looked at the sky, and said under his breath, with feeling, 'It is heavenly.' Back in the room he looked round, found the hammer, and hit the floor hard. While doing so, he mentioned that his canary, the one that was left [*after the other one had died*] was coming home, and he was looking forward to that. [*The bird had been at his nurse's house, who, as mentioned previously, lived with her husband in the neighbourhood, and whom he frequently saw.*]

Mrs K interpreted that he had intended by his hammering to open the door, to take out the dead babies, and to find the live ones, the bird which was coming home. [*A rather puzzling interpretation.*]

Richard went to the piano, which had been turned to the wall, and on which a number of things had been put, and said he would like to try to play. [*He had given up playing the piano after having reached quite an advanced development, playing sonatas and so on.*] In the course of the analysis, Richard had occasionally looked at the piano, but until then he had only once opened it and played a few notes (Fifth Session.) Now he attempted to open it and asked whether Mrs K could help him [*again, she must help him*] to move it and to take the things off the lid. She did so. There was a big Union Jack in the corner by the piano. Richard said that he was going to keep an eye on it, meaning that it might fall down. He first very hesitantly played on the piano with one finger only, then he stopped again. He said it was dusty. Could Mrs K help him dust it? She did so, and he tried playing again [*as though dusting, like cleaning the rust or dusting the little footstools, would improve his playing*], looking sad and saying that he had forgotten the sonatas he knew; then he tried something else, fetched a chair, sat down and played some harmonies of his own. He said, in a low voice, that he used to do this a lot.

After a while he asked whether Mrs K would play something, and she did so. [*Puzzling! and dangerous?*] Richard was very pleased, went back to the piano and, again trying some harmonies, said under his breath that this would be a great pleasure when he went home. [*Back to the house at Z after the war.*] He opened the top of the piano [*like opening the top of the baby tank*] and asked Mrs K to touch the keys while he looked 'inside'. He suddenly became aware of the word he had used and, glancing at Mrs K significantly, said, 'Again the inside.' Then he hit the keyboard with his elbow and trod hard on the pedals. He seized the Union Jack, enveloped himself in it, and noisily sang the National Anthem.

[*A rather gorgeous example of projective identification with the daddy's penis.*] His face was flushed, he was shouting and was trying to counteract anger and hostility by loyalty. [*She is not quite right about loyalty. Probably he is trying to counteract hostility by the promise of having a man's status some day.*] He looked out of the window, saw the old man opposite, and said 'There is the Bear.' [*Externalization of the penis invaded by projective identification.*] After a pause he asked whether Mr Smith had passed. So far he had paid hardly any attention to passers-by, but now tension and suspicion had set in and he began to watch out for them. [*The situation probably turned bad because of the juxtaposition of his incapacity and her capability. In playing for him she, as it were, exhibited the penis that she had inside her.*]

Mrs K interpreted the piano as standing for her inside, as Richard himself recognized, and his playing on it stood for his putting his genital into hers and for caressing her with his hands, as he had done earlier with the clock. [*The clock very clearly represents her mind and also the breast and probably the piano also has quite a lot to do with being in harmony with her and their minds working together.*]

From this point on the session goes progressively wrong as she pushes the theme of reparation to the Mummy by giving her babies with his penis. The photograph material follows, apparently accompanied by hammering the floor and flooding the kitchen. The fiasco of Friday ensues, barely rectified by the fragmented material of Saturday.

CHAPTER FIFTEEN

Fifteenth week: sessions 84–89

The concept of the combined object and its impact
on development

This fifteenth week is the least satisfactory of the whole analysis from the viewpoint of Mrs Klein's work. Richard is absolutely preoccupied with the approaching end, and attempts to work out the various possibilities, sometimes in quite a matter-of-fact and rather grown-up way. If she dies would somebody else be available? Could he not go to London, stay in a hotel? It seems to cause Mrs Klein great distress during the week and perhaps makes her work less well than usual. I would think that she must have been considering in her mind the same possibilities. She did call his mother, and try to discuss the question of the continuation of the analysis. Although she firmly took it upon herself that the decision to come to London was too dangerous for him, one assumes that she must have tried to investigate this with the mother and found her quite adamant about it. In a way Richard is better than Mrs Klein in this week, produces dreams and new play material, but does not get much in response. The previous week she had lost track of the formulation about the breast and the nipple and the upstairs and downstairs of the mummy's body. Things went wrong when she played the piano and later she lost her temper. But she was struggling.

Some of the notes to this week indicate conceptual limitations or difficulties she was having at that time. One such limitation is illustrated by the theme of the three conductresses, not only two, not just a pretty face and a not so pretty one, but now a painted-faced one as well. This third figure has to do with Richard's distrust of Mrs Klein and of his mother and his suspicion of hypocrisy. This is mainly a projection of his own hypocrisy and trickiness and slyness. The charm and seductiveness of the early weeks has been replaced by urgent clinging. He can hardly keep his hands off Mrs Klein now. He touches her and looks at her in a way in which his eyes are touching and clinging. The whole concept of clinging and sticking (which Mrs Bick has been investigating for the past few years) was unavailable to Mrs Klein. The difference between a baby holding on to the nipple in order to control the breast and a baby holding on to the nipple for fear of being dropped into the abyss seems to be very clearly illustrated by the situation with Richard at this point. At an infantile level he is in mortal dread of the end of his analysis as a precipice.

At the same time as being much more in contact with this very primitive anxiety which makes him so clinging, he is also noticeably more mature. His maturity shows not only in his actual social behaviour, like the cycling, his friendliness with John and John's friend, and in his way of dealing with the problem of trying to sort out the possibilities about the continuation of his analysis, but at one point he does actually think over the improvement that the analysis has brought into his mental life and he talks about it precisely and in detail. So these two can be seen to co-exist, infantile terror of being dropped and the beginnings of the young man who knows that he needs analysis if he is going to develop properly and does not want to be a dunce. A 'dunce' begins to take on the meaning of being unable to perform any useful function in the world, as illustrated in the material about the merchantmen carrying supplies to Alexandria.

The other way in which his anxiety is illustrated is the heart breaking little bit where he says, in despair, that he does not want to do anything, that it is lovely to do nothing. Mrs Klein is obviously hurt to hear this little boy express such apathetic cynicism.

He does come out of it very quickly and by contrast is at his most hopeful when he is reporting his dreams. Mrs Klein's analysis of it suggests that she thought it a somewhat manic hopefulness that tended to collapse again. But it is very interesting to see how important his dreams have become, implying that the acknowledgement of psychic reality had been re-established in him. The play with the keys, the darkening of the room, his reaction to the rain, are all a bit reminiscent of the early sessions and none of it has much substance in comparison with the dreams. It is noticeable that he shows very little reaction to the man coming in to read the meters. That spark of humour in him has an important link, as Mrs Klein points out, with the fact that there is always somebody who survives when there is a disaster. There is always a bit of life left. In the dream of the Black Island there is a little patch of green. Richard's capacity for humour is very closely linked with Mrs Klein's own spark, and is part of what saves him, whereas lapsing into apathy, 'it's lovely to do nothing' seems a bit connected with his father's state, which overshadows the week, with the renewed fear that he might die. Certainly Richard's tiredness seems very intimately connected with the father again being very tired.

But the main material of the week centres on the three conductresses, and the dreams are accordingly about buses and ships and cars. In the Tuesday session (page 430) Mrs Klein was talking about the three conductresses and describing the one with the painted face:

> Mrs K suggested that the conductress he liked stood also for Nurse. When he felt uncertain and suspicious about Mummy, he had turned to Nurse, who at that time was not married, which meant she had no husband as Mummy had. The pretty conductress stood for Mummy, who was prettier than Nurse; but there was a time when Richard loved Nurse more than Mummy, and he felt guilty about that. [*She is interpreting the conflict of loyalty in terms of the historical background.*]
> Richard said that Nurse was quite pretty – not at all ugly. He had seen her on the previous day when he changed buses on his journey home, and she had given him some sweets. (He now seemed to realize how fond he still was of her.) He said that Mrs K was not the one with the 'painted face'; she

was very pretty too, but not as pretty as Mummy. [*Trying to balance it amongst these women – the Judgment of Paris.*] Then he asked whether Mrs K felt hurt. Mrs K suggested that she represented a mixture of Mummy and Nurse.

Richard said that he had had a dream which was frightening but thrilling at the same time. A few nights before he also had a dream about two people putting their genitals together. He greatly enjoyed reporting the more recent dream and described it vividly and dramatically, sounding sinister at the frightening points, while at the climax his eyes were shining, and happiness and hope were expressed on his face: 'He saw Mrs K standing at at the bus stop in the village where the bus leaves for Y. But the bus was going to some other place; in the dream it went to Y only once every fortnight. It passed by without stopping.' (Here Richard made vivid noises like the bus passing by.) 'Richard ran after it to catch it, but the bus had gone. He went after all, but in a caravan. With him travelled a very happy family. The father and mother were middle-aged; there were quite a lot of children, and all of them were nice. They passed an island. With them was also a very big cat. First the cat bit his dog, but then they got on well together. Then the new cat chased his actual cat, but they also got to like each other. This new cat was not an ordinary cat, but it was very nice. It had teeth like pearls and it was more like a human being.'

Mrs K asked whether it was more like a woman or like a man. Richard replied it was both like a gentleman and a nice woman. He said: 'The island was on a river. On the bank of the river the sky was quite black, the trees were black, there was sand which was sand-coloured but the people were also black. There were all sorts of creatures, birds, animals, scorpions, all black; and all of them, people and creatures, were quite still. It was terrifying.' [*The stillness, not so much the blackness, was terrifying.*] Richard's face expressed horror and anxiety. [*In the Wolf Man's dream it was also the stillness of the wolves in the tree which was so terrifying. Freud interpreted that as representing in reverse the violent motion of the parents in intercourse.*]

Mrs K asked what the island was like. Richard said the island was not quite black, but the water and sky around were. There was a patch of green on the island and the sky over the island showed a little blue. The stillness was terrible. Suddenly Richard called out, 'Ahoy there', and at that moment everybody and everything became alive. He had broken a spell. They must have been enchanted. People began to sing; the scorpions and other creatures jumped back into the water, everybody was overjoyed, everything turned light, the sky became all blue.

Mrs Klein's interpretation of the dream emphasizes the reparative impulse from the manic viewpoint and the light goes out of Richard's eyes. She does not see a link to his calling for help so frequently nor its resemblance to the child in the Colette–Ravel operetta calling 'Mamma'. Clearly she thinks the 'Ahoy there' is similar to his kicking the buildings up again with his jack-boots. She does not think that his new-found friendliness is breaking the spell, friendliness generated by the happy internal (caravan) family and the earlier (by two days) Adam and Eve dream. The dream may be representing the possibility that when Mrs Klein goes away as a external object (connected with the buses and the conductresses and the bus not waiting for him) that an internal experience of family may continue to generate friendliness and happiness in him.

The puzzling notes to this session go some distance to explain the difficulty on a conceptual basis, relating to the interaction of internal with external situations, with special reference to the combined object. (Note II, p. 433):

Richard had at that point shown a step in development: he was able to feel that he and I, representing his mother, could be together without his internal object or my internal object interfering. A good balance between internal and external situations and relations is of fundamental importance. In Richard's case this meant that the combined parent figure – and his internal persecutors – had at least temporarily lost in power. [*It is not clear whether his 'internal persecutors' stand in apposition or in contrast to 'combined parent figure'.*] This was an indication of progress, although I am aware that these changes were not fully established.

What Mrs Klein seems to be saying is that in order to have a good relationship to an external object, there has to be a balance between it and the relationship to the internal object and that the internal object should not interfere too much. In ordinary terms that would mean something like 'your conscience should not bother you too much' but also must mean 'your internal object is not always clamouring for attention'. Now, if it is clamouring for attention it is a little bit hard to see how it manages to be a good combined internal object. It shows that at the most advanced point of her work at the end of the 1950s she was still not really decided about the role of the combined internal object – which meant father and mother together in intercourse, vagina and penis together, breast and nipple together as a sexual combination – whether this functioned as a good object or whether it functioned as too powerful an object that flooded the personality with sexual excitement, overpowered it with its activity, stirred envy and was in that way a disorganizing influence. In *Envy and Gratitude* she seemed to consider the combined object as the core of strength in the personality, but here in the notes I think she reveals that she was still quite uncertain about it because of the intensity of the envy that this combined object is felt to arouse. Richard's Adam and Eve dream, a primal scene dream, visualizes the parents and their genitals but he does not seem to be shocked with envy or overwhelmed by sexual excitement. In fact, seeing their genitals looking so huge like the monster he described, is unpleasant. This dream is an important prelude to the Black Island dream with its hopefulness about this destruction being reversible in psychic reality: that dead objects, dead babies can be brought back to life by goodwill towards the good, creative intercourse of the internal parents.

Now this is related to Mrs Klein's uncertainty about the conceptual status of the depressive position. She had never absolutely crystallized this in her mind, for sometimes she speaks of 'penetrating' the depressive position, 'overcoming', 'surpassing', all of which have a different implications regarding the meaning of 'depressive position'. This is brought out in note no. 4, on page 434:

Here we are touching on one of the important anxiety situations inherent in the depressive position. If Richard felt himself to be full of attacked and therefore bad objects (for instance, the dangerous, attacked flies and the lobster) and dangerous excrement, as well as destructive impulses, then the good objects inside him appeared to be endangered. [*Are these attacked, damaged objects different from bad objects produced by splitting-and-idealization?*] This meant in states of great anxiety that everything inside him was dead. Richard tried to solve this problem by taking out the bad and dangerous elements (the soot). But when he felt more secure, he resorted, as in the dream, to reviving and improving the bad objects. [*Omnipotently? it is not clear.*] It is interesting that the island had not been altogether black, but that there had been a patch of green and a bit of blue sky in the centre. This centre of goodness, which enabled him to keep hope going, thus represented the good breast, the good analyst, and the good nurse, as well as the good parents, in harmony [*intercourse?*]; and from this core of goodness life and reparation could spread. [*Life and reparation would seem then, to spread from 'the core of goodness', the internal object not the self.*] The play with the train and the baby on the swing had shown that the good baby also stood for regaining and preserving life. (As mentioned before, Richard was extremely fond of young babies and often asked his mother to have a child. When she replied that she was too old, he said that this was nonsense, of course she could have babies, and there is little doubt that he assumed the same of the analyst.)

The good breast as the core of the ego I take to be a fundamental precondition for ego development. Richard had always maintained his belief in the light-blue Mummy. The idealized mother co-existed with the persecutory and suspect one. Nevertheless, idealization was based on a feeling [*not a psychological fact*] of having internalized the good primal object to some extent, and this was his mainstay in all his anxieties. In the present stage of the analysis, Richard's capacity to integrate the ego and to synthesize the contrasting aspects of his objects had clearly increased and he had become more able, in phantasy [*not in psychic reality*] to improve the bad objects and to revive and re-create the dead ones [*all of this sounds like an active process by the ego and not something that happens to it through the mysterious agency of 'the core of goodness'*]; this, in turn, linked with hate being mitigated by love. [*Mitigate by love implies something meaningful, rather than mechanical as in Freud's use of 'neutralize'*.] In the dream, Richard could also bring the two parents together in a harmonious way.

These processes were, however, not fully successful, as was shown by my being left behind when I was hidden behind the man, which represented Richard's doubts as to whether the union of the parents would actually be good. (This indicated again the combined parent figure.)

Clearly Mrs Klein was not really decided whether this combined parent figure represented the core of the ego and of ego strength or whether 'in harmony' meant two parents with a possibility of combination. Therefore she remained uncertain about the breast and the nipple being in itself essentially a combined object. Her approach to the dreams seems, therefore, to hedge a little bit in favour of hauling Richard into the latency period, that is, rather encouraging him to desexualize his objects, to have the nice middle-aged parents in the nice caravan with the nice children and the cats love each other and so do the dogs, even if they occasionally bite each other.

The whole thing is being suburbanized with niceness. In the same way she wants him to play the piano. Everyone wants him to play the piano but that was not her technique. At this point in the analysis, in this week in particular, she was not at her best. She docs not make much of the poppy and the little fir cone. She docs not make much of the dreams. She has missed the opportunity to show him how frightened he is of dying and that the end of the analysis means, for the baby part of him, the danger of blackness spreading everywhere. Perhaps she could not bring herself to frighten him that much. But, more important, Mrs Klein did not have the conceptual equipment. The issues about which she was uncertain are still unclear, or perhaps essentially mysterious: the clinging; the fear of blackness; the 'dead end'.

CHAPTER SIXTEEN

Sixteenth week: sessions 90–93

The achievements of the analysis, with special reference to dependence on internal objects

The material that Richard brings in these four days is less dramatic than the previous week with exception of the lovely piece about the umbrella with which Mrs Klein works so beautifully. He tends mainly to peregrinate round different types of material that he brought earlier on in the analysis and a little bit of a dream or really the extension of the dream that he brought on the previous Saturday. In a sense there is nothing very new, no expectation on either part of discovering anything else during these last sessions.

It is all a rather sad reviewing of what they had accomplished and some attempt at making more explicit what they have not accomplished. Richard cannot keep his hands off Mrs Klein and these hands that are caressing and touching her also turn into the crab's claws waiting to fasten on her. This is the clinging material which Mrs Klein had no conceptual framework for developing, but the fear of falling comes out in the parachute material and is discussed in the notes connected with it. It gives an insight into a fundamental insecurity of an extremely primitive sort, underlying the weakness of Richard's ego and his distrust of his mother. This distrust is connected with the dark-blue mummy, this pretty conductress whom he says he 'wouldn't have'. But one can see that his mother, like the conductress who is accused of saying 'stand up', is the mother who expected too much of him in some way, expected him to be too independent, too manly, too potent. Mrs Klein also has tended, in emphasizing his genital conflicts, his castration anxiety, his wish to put his penis into the mummy and explore her inside, expected too much masculinity from him. Something very strongly feminine has not been allowed to develop and perhaps has not fared much better during this analysis, although he has had an opportunity to express it occasionally.

At the end of the Saturday session there had been the dream of the empty bus, to which Richard brings more detail on Monday; again the eerie stillness, as in the Black Island dream, is central. *The bus slowed down when Richard rang the bell and he jumped out while it was still moving*, which is a very clear indication that the analysis is still a going concern for him. He feels it to be cut off at a time when he is probably making his greatest progress.

Beside the bus in the dream *there was a flattened car in which a little girl was lying next to her father, but then she turned into a spaniel*. The flattened car seems to link with an earlier piece of material in which Richard closes the frame of Mrs Klein's clock, so that it almost collapsed, and then, saying that he was still supporting it, opens it quickly and says 'Now she is all right again'. I think that is a very important link to the dream. The little girl in the flattened car has something to do with his own femininity which in this brief analysis had very little opportunity to come into much contact with Mrs Klein but has remained in the projected state, in his mother or Mrs Klein or perhaps even the little red-haired girl or the bus conductress. It would thus have the significance of an unborn sister.

These seem to me to be the indications from the dreams and from his attitude towards the conductress, that there has been too much expectation about his masculinity and not enough recognition of his femininity. On the other hand, the extraordinary progress at infantile level is beautifully tied up in the umbrella-parachute material on Tuesday (p. 455):

Richard appeared not to have listened to Mrs K's interpretation. But at this point he again emphatically confirmed that he did not want to hurt Mrs K in any way. Yet a minute later he threw all the buses except the 'electric train bus', which stood for himself, down from the table, saying that it was a 'precipice'. [*Here is the falling theme, the abyss.*] His face was flushed and he was very excited. But he was at once concerned when he saw that the two front wheels of the engine had come off, and asked Mrs K whether she was angry and whether she could mend it.

Mrs K said that she could mend it and interpreted Richard's wish to know whether he had actually done harm to her children and friends, and if so, could she make them well again and forgive Richard for his hate.

Richard went into the kitchen, drew several buckets of water, and said that this water was not very clean; but apparently he did not mind this. He added that he wanted to draw all the water so that the tank should become clean. While drawing water, he kept on looking into the tank to see how the water whirled into the pipe and took the dirt with it.

Mrs K interpreted that Richard was expressing his desire to clean her inside and Mummy's inside from bad 'big job', babies, and genitals. His attacks on Mrs K, represented by the goods train, were meant predominantly to free her from the bad Hitler-Daddy – the ammunition which was put on top of the train – and to save and protect her. But he was also jealous of her, just as he was when he thought of Daddy being in bed with Mummy while he was left by himself. This was why he had thrown the buses down the 'precipice'. The rival buses stood for the rival Daddy (also the good one) and for Paul and all the children who he thought might yet be born.

Richard had during the last few minutes played with Mrs K's umbrella which he had opened. He made it spin round and said he liked it. Then he used it as a parachute with which he was supposed to float down. He looked at the trademark and stated with satisfaction that it was British-made. Then, again, holding it open, he turned round and round with it and said that he was dizzy, he did not know where it was taking him. He also said over and over again that 'the whole world was turning round'. Then he let the umbrella drop gently; he once more said that it was a parachute and that he was not sure whether it would go down the right way. He told Mrs K that he had completely wrecked Mummy's best umbrella when he had used it as a parachute on a windy day. She had been 'speechless with rage'.

[*Here comes a gorgeous interpretation.*] Mrs K interpreted the umbrella as her breast; that it was British-made meant that it was a good breast, and that Mummy's breast was a good breast too. She referred to his doubts about what Mrs K contained – a good or bad Mr K. The open umbrella stood for the breast, but the stick in it stood for Mr K's genital. Richard did not know whether he could trust this breast when he took it in because it was mixed with Mr K's genital, just as in his mind his parents and their genitals were mixed inside him. The question where the umbrella would take him expressed his uncertainty whether they were controlling him inside or not. [*This is her point about the combined objects being too powerful and controlling.*] The world which was turning round was the whole world he had taken into himself when he took in the breast – or rather Mummy mixed with Daddy, and her children, and all she contained. He felt the internalized powerful Daddy penis – the secret weapon – as something which made him powerful if he used it against an external enemy. But it became dangerous if it attacked and controlled him internally. Nevertheless, he trusted Mummy and Daddy – the umbrella – more than previously, both as external people and inside him. That was also why he now treated Mrs K's umbrella more carefully than he had formerly treated Mummy's.

That is incredibly condensed and really pulls together the whole treatment of this boy. In the second note to this material she writes (p. 457):

During the present session, apart from watching Mr Smith when he passed, Richard had hardly paid any attention to people on the road. He was deeply concentrated on an internal situation and in that respect he felt more secure than formerly. This more secure internal situation included a stronger belief in the good protective breast expressed by the parachute which had helped him in an emergency. Although it soon appeared that the good breast was mixed in his mind with the penis, nevertheless it seemed more reliable than on former occasions. [*But surely the umbrella would not function at all without the central stick-penis.*] More recently Richard had become able to direct his aggressiveness more consistently against the bad, the Hitler-father and to unite with the good mother and help her to defend herself. Instead of quickly turning his aggression against the breast when anxiety came up [*very crucial with this boy*], he could in a relatively more stable way maintain his trust in the breast and in the mother, and face the fight with the father [*that is the bad Hitler-father*] ... The change from stronger depression in the previous session to greater security in the present one was also due to a manic element in his mood. He used the stronger belief in the good internal Mrs K and mother, and the good father, to ward off the fear of parting and his depression. [*This is part of what she means by the use of manic defences as a modulating device in relation to depressive anxieties. A certain manic overestimation of the internal situation as a defence against being overwhelmed by external difficulty can also be reversed when external situations are good, to overcome anxiety about the internal situation, such as in the face of illness.*]

The next bit, which is so interesting, shows how Mrs Klein worked with internal situations. This is just after Richard has been making some demands about changes of time because he wanted to go with John Wilson. Mrs Klein could not accommodate him (p. 458):

Richard, at one moment when both trains were standing in the station, suddenly said he felt unwell and had a pain in his tummy. He looked pale.

Mrs K interpreted the station as Richard's inside. He expected all the time a collision inside him between the electric train, containing Mrs K and the good Mummy, and the hostile goods train, standing for all the angry patients and children from whom Richard wanted to take Mrs K away and run with her to his home town. [*That is her foundation for the interpretation of his illness – that he has been pursued in this play, as in the outside world, by all the daddies and all the children from whom he has taken the breast and mummy as his exclusive possession.*] Therefore he also wanted to change the time of his sessions, which meant taking Mrs K away from everybody else. While Richard was striving to avoid a collision between the trains, because he did not wish to hurt Mrs K and Mummy, and their children and wanted to finish the analysis peacefully, he did not seem to believe that he could avoid the collision internally. [*Here she should be linking it with his masturbation, which, for some reason, she always leaves out.*] This meant that he and Mrs K would be hurt or damaged by his rivals. Therefore he had seemed so tense during this play and had a tummy ache. [*She is interpreting this as an internal anxiety situation, experienced as an actual pain in his tummy, not a hypochondriacal situation.*]

Richard said, looking at Mrs K in surprise, 'The pain has now quite gone – why?' The colour had come back into his face.

Finally, on page 461, note III declares Mrs Klein's understanding of the structure of Richard's illness as well as the dynamics of his anxieties: 'I had already interpreted that one part of his self [*not ego*] 'felt to be good and allied with the good object, was fighting his destructive part combined with' [*not merely 'allied with' – that is, in projective identification*] 'the bad objects'. [*The bad objects produced by splitting-and-idealization.*]

This was the nature of his conflict with the Hitler-Daddy. But Mrs Klein was not able to differentiate that persecution from the paranoia towards Cook and Bessie. The paranoia had the structure of a destructive part of the self combined with – in projective identification with – the idealized part-objects, the breasts. This is perhaps the classical structure of paranoia.

There remains the task of briefly recapitulating the treatment of Richard. He started as a child who presented difficulties both characterological and symptomatic. We know that he was ineducable by virtue of being riddled with agoraphobic and claustrophobic anxieties and fear of other children. His character was freighted with insincerity and hypocrisy and pseudo-charm.

At the start of his analysis, his illness seems to have him in its grip and casts him back in his development, mainly during his schooldays in connection with his competitiveness with other boys, which resulted in his being bullied. It was undoubtedly aggravated by the war situation and by the bombing of the home, their moving and Paul going into the army.

During the course of this analysis, the transference process seems to have moved through a genital seduction period which quickly deepened into voyeuristic jealousy (the starfish draw-ings) and catastrophic masturbatory phantasy (the toy play). The struggle with rivals for the possession of the mother (empire drawings) began to generate depressive anxieties, and a period of intense oscillation of depression and persecution ensued which gave promise of an unresolvable distrust of the mother. This was surprisingly broken by the revelation of a focus of paranoid confusion between good and bad at the oral level [Cook and Bessie material] and the transference moved into high gear as Mrs Klein began to respond to the helpless baby in Richard. Splitting-and-idealization of self and objects (the trial dream and lightning drawings) began to improve in clarity as the end of the analysis hove in sight. Desperate clinging to the breast (touch-ing and drinking behaviour) and acceptance of it as a combined object (parachute-umbrella) strengthened his hopefulness about the strength and goodness of the internal situation, so long as he could be friendly to the other babies and not kill them (the milk-tank material and the Black Island dream.)

The paranoid-schizoid and depressive positions[1]

The subject I have been asked to talk about today is for many the most central of the psychoanalytic developments linked with the name of Melanie Klein. As with all psychoanalytic concepts it seems to me that, to understand their significance, we have to put them in the context of their history. And studying the history of Mrs Klein's ideas is different from studying that of Freud, owing to the fact that Freud is both a clinician and a theoretician, whilst Mrs Klein is almost exclusively a clinician who describes far more than she theorizes.

The evolution of Freud's thought is like a country that underwent two revolutions: the first being the fall of the theory of hysteria, and the second being the overthrow of the theory of the libido in the 1920s and its substitution by the structural theory. The work of Melanie Klein on the other hand has grown in a way more analogous to the peaceful transformation that is characteristic of English political institutions. It seems to me that Melanie

---

[1] A talk given in Novara in 1974, published in *Quaderni di Psicoterapia Infantile* (1975), edited by C. Brutti and F. Scotti, pp. 125–41. Translated by Adrian Williams. Also published, with a discussion, in *Adolescence: Talks and Papers* by Donald Meltzer and Martha Harris (2011) [Ed.].

Klein, not having a particularly theoretical mentality, did not particularly take account of the changes that were taking place in her use of terminology, and the theoretical implications that she was putting forward.

First I shall describe a way of viewing the conceptual changes that lay behind the formulation of the paranoid-schizoid and depressive positions, and then I shall link these to the problem of how to deal with adolescence as a period marked by specific points of change: first the transition from latency to puberty, then the transition from puberty to adolescence, and finally the transition from adolescence to adulthood. Let me underline some theoretical elements that help us to understand these transitions, and then describe the clinical implications of a move from the paranoid-schizoid to the depressive position, after which we can discuss technical problems occurring in clinical work.

Melanie Klein entered psychoanalytic practice in 1919–1920 just at the time when Freud was starting to change the libido theory into what would later become the structural theory of psychoanalysis. It is important to try to see how the work of these two people links up and also how it is different. The fundamental difference is that Freud's approach was essentially a way of understanding psychopathology, and reconstructed infancy in retrospect; whilst Melanie Klein's approach originated in her interest in the development of babies, and then investigated the connection between this and the psychopathology of adult life. The reconstruction of infancy made by Freud lacks something which actual babies in their relation to the world could demonstrate in flesh and blood. The work of Melanie Klein on the other hand makes too little distinction between evolutionary conflicts and pathological processes.

When Mrs Klein started work in the 1920s, as we know, she began by observing the development of babies and then gradually adapted the psychoanalytic method to the treatment of children. At that time, in terms of theory, she was working primarily with Freud's ideas as modified by Abraham. These included the progression of the erogenous zones, and the pregenital organization and then genital organization of the libido; and at this time pregenital also meant pre-oedipal. At this time Freud or more particularly Abraham retained the idea that the Oedipus complex only started in the genital phase of the evolution of the libido. Thus the first contribution of Melanie Klein to analysis falls into two categories: the first (for many the most important) was her discovery that babies are much preoccupied with internal spaces of the body, particularly of the mother and of themselves. Freud never conceptualized this. The second (as a result of babies' interest in these spaces) was the new concreteness given to the concepts of introjection and projection that Freud had already described. Melanie Klein was thus able to delineate the phenomena that she called the 'early Oedipus complex'. This was different from Freud's view not only in its description of a stage earlier than the development of partial objects, but also because it gave a greater psychic reality to internal objects than either Freud or Abraham had been able to fully conceptualize.

In the course of this Mrs Klein noted the sadism of babies, which gave her the impression that these phenomena began in the earliest stages of infancy, and she started to use the term 'position' for the first time. At first she used it in a variety of ways. She mentions a depressive position, an obsessive position, a maniacal position, a paranoid position. By the last she seems to refer to the anxieties connected with sadism and specifically organization of defences against these anxieties. At this stage in her thinking the term 'position' is used almost exclusively in a descriptive sense, and is applied to almost any type of anxiety and defence related to the two periods of intense sadism of early infancy: oral-sadistic and anal-sadistic. In 1930, writing on manic-depressive states, Klein started to use the term in a more specific way, and in the two papers on manic and depressive states (Klein 1935, 1940), she used the term 'position' in a way that linked with Freud's theory of fixation points, to describe certain states as points of fixation peculiar to schizophrenia and manic depression.

In this period (the 1930s) she was talking of three positions: paranoid, depressive, and manic; and I think that at this time she maintained explicitly that in these respects the mental state of babies is fundamentally the same as that of adults. This one can say is the psychopathological phase of the use of the term 'position'. Klein talked of babies who 'overcome' the position in a way analogous to the way Freud talks of 'working through'. She tended to talk as though babies suffer from illness equivalent to schizophrenia, mania and depression, and was criticized for having concluded that babies suffer from mental illness. By the time she wrote 'Notes on some schizoid mechanisms' in 1946, her use of the term 'position' was becoming restricted to 'paranoid position' and 'depressive position'. Gradually she started to join paranoid with schizoid, differentiating it thereby from Fairbairn's concepts. Refining her picture of the emotional qualities of these positions, she became less exclusively preoccupied with sadism and its consequences and came instead to refer to love for the primary object in order to distinguish the states of mind which are preoccupied with the good health and survival of the object, not only of the baby.

So she began to describe the central nucleus of the depressive position in terms of 'pining' – a feeling of loneliness, mourning, regret, and awareness of separation. This seems to me to be a very important turning point in her thinking: added to the idea of love in the depressive position as centring on the object rather than the self. Such a change brought to psychoanalysis a vision of love which has no place in Freud's theories, which were from the beginning based on the idea of gratification of the libido.

Later Klein hypothesized that love might triumph over the narcissistic impoverished libido, consequently benefiting the ego. So while the first use of 'position' was an evolutionary one linked to the idea of defence, and the second use was linked essentially to psychopathology and the concept of fixation, the use of the term in the 1940s and thereafter placed such concepts in a field that one might call 'economic'.

But this also changes completely the meaning of the economic concept in metapsychology. For Freud, an economic concept was about quantitative aspects of the distribution of the libido and its vicissitudes. Its roots lay in his neurophysiological model of the mind and in the idea of quantities of excitement. One of the revolutionary elements one finds in Freud is his determination to establish a mental science free from moralistic pre-judgements; and in his efforts to avoid assigning a particular *weltanschauung* to psychoanalysis one might say he proceeded in a manner that was non-moralistic to the point of being cynical. This is not to say that in his clinical work he was cynical or amoral; in studying his clinical cases, in particular the Rat Man, it is evident that his work is completely free from cynicism. Notwithstanding this, right to the end of his life – even after the new theory of the life and death instincts – he tended to try to integrate psychoanalytic thinking with biology in a way that might eliminate any philosophical standpoint or almost any idea of values.

It seems to me that the initial work of Melanie Klein faithfully follows this pattern: in her description of sadism in babies there is not the slightest trace of moral preoccupation. The baby's pain is seen as deriving exclusively from the feeling of persecution; the conflict between love and hate is related almost exclusively to the wellbeing and happiness of the baby; and the child that is exercising his sadistic impulses (in reality or in imagination) suffers from persecutory anxieties. In Klein's original idea of the depressive position, he seeks to escape these feelings of persecution by making 'restitution' as she called it. This meant essentially to give back what he had stolen and put together what he had broken. Gradually 'restitution' turned into 'reparation'; and reparation meant repairing the damage in order to avoid persecutory anxiety.

In the second phase of her use of the term 'position'—the psychopathology phase—Klein uses 'reparation' in a way which makes it indistinguishable from that which she afterwards called 'manic reparation'. She specified that this manic reparation is motivated essentially by omnipotence.

In the third phase of the use of the 'positions', beginning with writings on mourning and continuing with those on schizoid mechanisms, there is a slow and gradual change. By the time of *Envy and Gratitude* (1957) and 'On loneliness' (1963) the entire approach has changed. The paranoid-schizoid and depressive positions start to lose their evolutionary specificity. She no longer describes them as something which occurs at the third month of life and resolves around the time of weaning, but starts to consider them as a type of mental conflict which has its origin around the third month but continues for the entire life of the individual.

The depressive position therefore is no longer described as something which is to be overcome, but something which is entered into. The movement between paranoid-schizoid and depressive positions begins to be seen as a continuous oscillation in the sense later delineated sharply by Dr Bion as Ps<–>D. The concept of love is modified to mean that concern for the wellbeing of the object, predominates over concern for the comfort of the self.

I have said this is an economic concept, but a qualitative one. This does not in my view replace the quantitative economic concepts described by Freud, but is in addition to them. If one takes the economic concepts and tries to put them in meaningful order, one would put it like this: the most primitive economic concept is the repetition compulsion; this is the main economic principle of the id, that knows nothing other than the repetition of previous experience and past activity, directly connected with physiological processes. The pleasure principle modified by the reality principle is the main economic principle used by the ego in its attempt to govern relations with the id, as distinct from the external world. This is, one could say, purely narcissistic, in the sense of Freud's 'primary narcissism'.

But the paranoid-schizoid and the depressive position are the main economic principles of relations with the object. The paranoid-schizoid position is a value system in which the health, security and pleasure of the self dominate, whilst the depressive position is a value system in which the health, security and happiness of the object prevail. So in the later work of Mrs Klein the paranoid-schizoid and depressive positions have no special tie to evolutionary phases of development, nor any specific tie to pathological configurations; they are of general economic reference to all developmental phases and all psychopathological configurations. The concept of reparation also takes on a new significance, not as something that the baby is able to do actively, but as something which he permits to happen by restraining his destructive impulses. Reparation comes to be the precise opposite of destructive impulses and is connected very directly with the concept of integration.

In her paper of 1946 on schizoid mechanisms, Melanie Klein describes the two principal techniques by means of which disintegration comes about – through splitting processes, and through projective identification. These are truly named 'schizoid' mechanisms, and are the means by which the paranoid-schizoid position comes to be built. Reparation may be considered the principal depressive mechanism and in many ways the neutralization of schizoid mechanisms. Thus that which has been split in schizoid mechanisms is reunited, and that which has been projected through projective identification is taken back inside.

These are the active components of the depressive position and are accompanied by depressive pains of various types: they form a spectrum that extends from feelings of regret, remorse, guilt at one end, to feelings of loneliness, depression, and pain at separation, at the other. She came to hypothesize that the self, when it becomes capable of playing its part in reparation, puts back together that which has been split inside itself, and recovers parts that had been projected outside, suffering feelings of depression because of the damage it had done; whilst at the same time, owing to the feeling of loneliness, it now experiences the objects as separate from the self and this triggers a reciprocal reparation. This situation in which the self reunites split parts and suffers depressive pain, while the parental figures are separate from the self and united in a reparative sexual rapport, is opposed to the paranoid-schizoid conception of the primal scene in which the self intrudes into the parents' sexual union and stimulates a state of excitement, envy and jealousy in which schizoid mechanisms are operative.

With this conception of the paranoid-schizoid and depressive positions as the main economic principles that regulate and one might say direct the developmental processes, one can from the clinical point of view examine almost any developmental crisis in terms of transitions and oscillations between paranoid-schizoid and depressive positions. This is the meaning of Bion's little diagram Ps<–>D with the double arrows. And it is from this point of view that we wish to examine the processes of transition that they illuminate between puberty, adolescence and adult life.

Before going on I will highlight some points of delicate equilibrium between the paranoid-schizoid and the depressive positions. One concerns the use of the term 'guilt'. Guilt as it appears in depressive anxiety is rather more serious than regret or remorse, and probably involves the fear of having caused irreparable damage to the object. Guilt brought to light clinically in the analytic situation tends to be seen as persecutory guilt, and links with Freud's concept of the cruelty of the superego that results from quantities of aggressive impulse generated by the self. Klein has described this in more detail from the structural point of view. The cruel superego that produces persecutory guilt may derive from three sources: the first being splitting and idealization of the object into idealized object and persecutory object.

The second source of persecutory guilt is projective identification of the bad parts of the self into the object, maybe then recombining the bad part of the object with the bad part of the self. The third source derives from the damaged object: the object seen as damaged in an irreparable way by the sado-masturbatory attack. Gradually the work of Melanie Klein was developing, and reached its most evolved form in the *Narrative of a Child Analysis* (1961) and in *Envy and Gratitude* (1957). This last category of persecutory guilt, felt as having caused irreparable damage of the object, seems in her clinical descriptions to centre itself ever more closely on the killing of the babies inside the mother.

The other point of delicate balance in the relation between the paranoid-schizoid and the depressive positions concerns the concept of reparation. Of the four types of reparation, two seem to lend themselves to the description 'false'. One type is described very clearly by Melanie Klein as 'manic reparation' in which omnipotence is used to try to reverse the damage done to the objects. The second is another type of false reparation, connected with what Mrs Klein initially called 'restitution'; it is insincere, like stealing a bottle of wine, drinking it and handing back the empty bottle.[2]

The threshold of the depressive position

One of Mrs Klein's primary discoveries is that for the baby the body of the mother is equivalent to the world for the adult, whose view of the world is derived from this infantile rapport with the mother's body. The essence of the depressive position consists in being able to worry about envious attacks on the babies.

In every analysis our best chance of studying this oscillation between Ps and D is the place that I have called the 'threshold of the depressive position'. This is the most difficult moment in any analysis, when there is a crisis in the quality of the collaboration of which the patient is capable. This crisis helps us to better

---

[2] There follow extracts from the (incomplete) tape recording.

define a concept that Freud cites from time to time but which has not found a proper place in psychoanalytic thought: namely, the concept of introspection. A person has fully entered the depressive position only when he is able to recognize by means of introspection how much this process has cost his objects – not how much it would appear, but how much he actually feels to be the cost. This recognition implies that egocentricity has been overcome and converted into introspection. Different tensions are involved: the person becomes preoccupied not with sensations but with phantasies and motivation. When one has succeeded in bringing a patient to this threshold, where he can be handed over responsibility for his own feelings, motivation and phantasies, then he is ready to start the work of self-analysis.

The psychoanalytical process

I have described the paranoid-schizoid and depressive positions as 'economic' concepts, which determine the developmental process and the transition of the individual from one stage to another. I should like now to talk about the clinical application of these concepts.

In my book *The Psychoanalytical Process* I consider the psychoanalytic process itself as a sequence of developmental problems whose complexity correlates with the growing complexity of the organization of the mental apparatus. The moments of crisis and the crucial points of development become manifest here in confusions of every type, and the economic principles of the paranoid-schizoid and depressive positions regulate the quantitative and qualitative elements that are occurring at the time.

These confusions possess their own internal logic, which is specifically linked to the development of complex structures starting from more simple structures. The order of development is something like this: in the beginning is Klein's observation of the splitting and idealization that permits a differentiation (perhaps somewhat exaggerated) between good and bad. After this comes a confusion between self and object – and in my book I hold that the major interference in the process of development is the mechanism of projective identification. Next there comes what I call 'zonal confusion' between the different areas of the body, the different parts of the body of the object, and the functional rapport between them. This point of crisis corresponds in fact to the Oedipus complex described by Freud, and it is the problem of the combined object: it derives from the primitive relationship of breast and nipple when understood as a 'combined object'. And then, there is the problem of differentiating the infantile from the adult part, and the problem of introjective identification with the combined object.

From latency to adulthood

In the light of this sequence of confusions I would like now to examine the development from latency to adulthood, bearing in mind above all these problems of differentiation between good and bad, between self and object, between the zones; the problems of the Oedipus complex and the formation of the combined object; and finally the problem of the differentiation of the adult part from the infantile part of the personality.

As I have described in *The Psychoanalytical Process*, the development of analysis—like that of the individual in normal life—is not linear. It is more like a spiral in which the entire spectrum from good to bad, from adult to infantile, repeats continually and cyclically the gradual evolution of the mental apparatus. I should like to return for a moment to the nature of latency. According to Freud latency followed the Oedipus complex as a result of the internalization of the imagined parents and the definitive formation of the superego. According to Klein on the other hand the formation of the superego happens in a much more gradual way at a part-object level. The period of latency is thus not something that completes a phase of development; it is more like a defence constellation that produces a developmental arrest, a period of waiting that allows the child to relax its intense oedipal interest in the parents, and to go out into the external world and start to socialize and learn scholastically.

According to Klein there are particular defences in latency that silence the oedipus complex for some while, without actually resolving its obsessional mechanisms. Reading her first works it is not always easy to understand what she meant by 'obsessional mechanisms'. It became clearer from around 1930 especially with the paper on manic-depressive states (1935). Obsessional mechanisms are founded essentially on two operations: omnipotent control of the objects, and the separation of the parental objects in order to prevent the sexual union responsible for the violent feelings and conflicts of the Oedipus complex. The latency period enables psychic reality to be neglected in favour of interest in the external world. In consequence one sees a slowing up or reduction of emotionality and also therefore of imagination. It follows that the concept of good and bad – produced after the primitive splitting and idealization of self and object – takes on a certain rigidity, with a moralistic and legalistic flavouring. The latency organization of the personality presumably permits the child to be away from home without feeling overwhelmed by loneliness, jealous suspicion, and the sense of persecution. It permits him to interest himself in the world in a sufficiently obsessive way, manifest in the hunger for information and the desire to acquire skills of various types.

Whether or not this has biological roots in Freud's sense of repeating the glacial era in the development of the individual, or whether it is perhaps derived from cultural pressures via the influence of the parents who wish to prepare the child for school, is a problem we will leave for anthropological research. I believe the second theory and think that latency may be encouraged by parental pressure. Whatever the origin of latency, there is no doubt that its destruction by puberty is a biological process, directly linked with the emergence of sexual forces and desires. If we have the opportunity to observe clinically a child making the transition from latency to puberty we see how the burst of excitement in the transference absolutely breaks to pieces these obsessional mechanisms.

In puberty it seems the organization of the personality that had been built up during the first ten or eleven years of life suddenly reveals itself to be very fragile, falls to pieces and has to be newly constructed, intensifying the obsessional mechanisms. Thus in the transition from latency to puberty we can see a continuous oscillation in behaviour between that of a turbulent child and of a self-contained adult, in close sequence.

When this disintegration occurs, at puberty, it reactivates infantile confusions in an atmosphere very different of that from early infancy. First of all there is the difference caused by rapid growth, and the changes happening in the body. Secondly there is the change in the child's environment in which new space and liberty opens up to him. Thirdly there starts to emerge a community of children marked out from that of small children and of parents. The community of adolescents starts to emerge. It is in this context of the pubertal community, and even more of the adolescent community, that teenagers start to experience the major part of their emotional lives. One has the impression that in this phase of development processes of intense disintegration are repeated, typical of the paranoid-schizoid position, which from the point of view of dynamics link to the time just after weaning. Entry into the pubertal or adolescent community, the withdrawal of emotional ties from the community of parents and young children, may be directly linked to a phase of development in which the baby at the breast becomes simply one of the babies in the family.